God's Wonderful Woman:
The Process from Me to You

Kimberly D. Harris

God's Wonderful Woman:
The Process from Me to You

Copyright © Kimberly D. Harris

All Rights Reserved

All quotes from the Bible are from the King James Version

ISBN: 979-8-218-62140-7

DEDICATION

I dedicate this book back to my Lord and Savior, Jesus Christ! Because if it was not for him, I would not have this story to tell that would bring him glory. It is only because of him that I can present this to the world today.

I dedicate this book to my mother Geraldine Anthony. She's been there when I needed her and has supported me no matter what I went through. Even when she didn't understand me or the choices I made, she was always there, and she loved me no matter what I did or said. I'm so blessed that my momma is my momma. Love you, Momma!

I dedicate this book to my kids. They helped shape and mold me into God's wonderful woman. Each child served a purpose in my life, and I will never forget what they did for me and how they changed my life. My baby son, Keyon taught me how to accept life as it is and that you can make it through any circumstance with God. He came, lived, and died so that I could grow into who god called me to be. My oldest son, Keymonie showed unconditional love and loyalty towards me. My daughter, Kimmyah is teaching me every day that there is a greater purpose for my life. I aim to be a great example to her as a woman so that she may be able to carry on the legacy when I am gone from this earth.

CONTENTS

	Acknowledgments	i
1	In The Beginning	1
2	Rebellious Years	11
3	Not My Baby! Why My Baby! Thank God for My Baby!	25
4	The Shaping and Molding Years	63
5	The Shift	93
6	The Transformation	109

ACKNOWLEDGMENTS

I want to thank God for giving me everything I need to complete this book. I want to thank my mother, kids, and husband for being there throughout this process of writing this book. I want to thank my editor for her patience, kindness, and expertise on this book. I want to thank DNA Publishing for mentoring me and helping to get this book written and published.

1

IN THE BEGINNING

For I know the plans I have for you, declares the Lord, plans to prosper you and not to harm you, plans to give you hope and a future. Jeremiah 29:11

It all started with the plans that God had for me: the plans to prosper me, the plans to better me, the plans of hope for me and not to harm me. Even though I say it is God's plan, I sure felt the hurt and discomfort of it. But that hurt did not detract from his purpose that was planned for my life. His plans and will for my life shall be done on Earth as it is in heaven. You may be feeling the same way or have felt the same way at some point in your life. I want to remind you that God knows exactly where you are, and He knows how to get you to where He wants you to be. Your job is to trust God in the process, and you will prosper. God's plans for me started before I was born.

God's plans for me started before I was born. "Before I formed thee in the belly, I knew thee; and before thou camest forth out of the womb I sanctified thee, and I ordained thee a prophet unto the nations," Jeremiah 5:1. As you can see, God already knew you and all you would go through according to His plan for your life.

I grew up in a house on the west side of Indianapolis with my mom, grandmother, and two uncles. My granny allowed other family members to stay with us when they didn't have anywhere else to live. Home was fun because it was full of family. I attended public schools in our neighborhood, and we all attended the neighborhood church.

I can see now that I was moving with God's plan for me when I was just eight years old. My family and I attended Greater King Solomon Missionary Baptist Church in the late 1980s. It was a two-story white house renovated into a church in the middle of the neighborhood that smelled like old wet wood, and it was surrounded by abandoned houses in a drug-infested neighborhood. We would attend church every Sunday from nine in the morning to nine at night. Sunday mornings started with Sunday school then morning service. After morning service was dismissed, we all went home to Granny's house and ate Sunday dinner together as a family. Then we had to either go back to our church or go to another church for the afternoon and evening services.

I enjoyed going to Sunday school because of the glazed

donuts and orange juice. Ha! Those thoughts as children were so innocent. As a child coming up, we had to find some kind of enjoyment in all the services we had to attend. Because when I was coming up in church, we didn't have a children's ministry as we do in churches today. We would all be in the sanctuary with our parents and grandparents trying not to fall asleep and risk getting a whooping in church.

One Sunday morning, the deacons made the altar call. This is where you come to Jesus to be saved, or you are coming up for prayer. After we had prayer at the altar, if you wanted salvation or to dedicate your life to Christ, you'd sit in the chair. Then, the deacons ask the person in the chair a few questions. After the questions, the person in the chair confesses aloud that Jesus is Lord and that they believe in their heart that God raised Him from the dead. After that, the person is saved and the whole church rejoices. Because now when you die your soul will go to heaven instead of hell.

As we were standing at the altar, I felt a push on the right side of me. The push felt so real I looked to see who pushed me, but no one was there. It was like a friend pushing you and telling you to sit right there! The push caused me to take notice of the chair, and then I had a desire to sit in it. When I sat in the chair during altar call one of my cousins also followed me and sat in the other chair. Then the deacons came over and asked the questions, and we confessed with our mouths that Jesus is Lord! We believed in our hearts that God raised Him from the dead. My cousin and I are saved now! Everyone in the sanctuary rejoiced and praised God for our salvation!

My cousin and I were about eight years old when we were baptized. Growing up, our family treated us like twins. We were born four days apart, and we did everything together as kids. Our parents dressed us alike and even styled our hair alike. We went to the same schools until we got older. I guess it was only right that we got saved together since we did everything else together.

As I look back at that time in my life, I may not know what was happening back then but one thing I did know was that I was saved, and I was not going to hell. Because when you were a child back then you only thought you were saved if you were baptized. But now as an adult and after I read the word for myself, I learned that it is when you confess it with your mouth and believe in your heart that you are saved. Just like the push I felt as a kid, I know now as an adult that was a push from the Holy Spirit, and God was calling me at an early age to give my life to Him.

God's plan was already operating in me. I was leading people to Christ and didn't even know about the anointing over my life. That just goes to show that God called and knew us before we entered our mother's womb. For God knows the purpose and plans He has for my life, not to harm me but to prosper me and give me a future. The Bible says in Romans 8:30 *And those he predestined, he also called, those he called, he also justified; those he justified he also glorified.* I thank God for calling me to him that Sunday and revealing himself to me. I am so grateful that he had me on his mind. Hallelujah!

I'll keep repeating this scripture because it brings me hope!

When things look strange, that scripture encourages me. It tells me that God knows where I am in life and that this trial is not to harm me, but it is working together for my good.

When I was about ten years old, I received the Holy Spirit one Sunday morning. The spirit was high, people were praising God, and the choir was singing "Jesus how I love calling your name." Next thing I knew, my legs began to shake. I then bent over crying trying to control what was happening to me and hide from others. At that age, it's hard to understand what is happening, especially when you're the only child who seems to be experiencing this. I couldn't fight it any longer, and now my body was visibly rocking and moving from side to side. My legs were shaking uncontrollably as I jumped up, hands lifted, calling on the name of Jesus with tears rolling down my face. This was the first time the Holy Spirit rested on me and the first time my family had seen a young person my age praising and shouting all over the church. But it was not the last time the Holy Spirit came up to me.

I remember the Holy Spirit would come upon me on Sunday mornings when I would be singing in the choir or even when my family had to go sing at different churches for special occasions. My mother, her sisters, and her cousins had a singing group called the Thomas Specials, and they would sing all over the city at different churches. As kids, we had to go and sometimes, the Holy Spirit would show up there. I was the only child shouting and praising God out of all the children who were at the services. All the other kids would just look at me watching to see what I would do next. They thought I didn't know that they were talking about me, but I could hear them saying to one another "Is she crying? What's wrong with her? She is about to start shouting!" I could feel them moving and getting out of the way. When I was done shouting, some of them would laugh and some would look at me with fear or amazement. God was calling me out at a young age and setting me apart early.

God anointed me, and he let everyone see that I was one of

His chosen ones. Maybe that was when the enemy entered the hearts of my cousins to be envious of me, and they didn't even know why. I still can't figure that out, but I'll touch on that later.

Meanwhile I was experiencing God in a way I never felt before. Not one adult talked to me about what was happening to me in church. No one ever told me that after the Holy Spirit comes upon you that you shall receive power. No one ever told me that there was a calling on my life, and God was going to use me. As a young child going through this and experiencing God in such a way, I needed an explanation and guidance. We need wisdom and understanding as we go through life. That could be one of the reasons why some young people stray away from church and God. They have a lack of understanding, and no one steps up to lead them on their journey. We are too busy or can't discern what God is doing in the life of others.

Because they lack knowledge and understanding of who God is, a lot of people nowadays hesitate to teach youth the knowledge or to mentor them on their journeys with Christ because of their own fear of being outshined. Young people need adults to help them and guide them, as well as pray for them while they are on this Christian path. We also need to encourage them to keep coming to church and to keep God first in their lives.

This helps them to get through tough times and challenging days. God is calling His people back to him no matter their age. God said a child shall lead. But how can they lead if we don't help them? Not one adult around me taught me about the power of God or even recognized that I was called and anointed.

It is so like God to put you around people who don't understand you. These same people will not know how to deal with you and the anointing that is over your life and if they did, they would never acknowledge it. Sometimes I think they didn't have the wisdom or understanding to explain to me or even guide me through this.

As a kid I kept going to church because my mom made me. I would sing in the choir and shout on some Sundays, and then I went back to school on Monday. I repeated that week after week. There was no reading the Bible, no Wednesday night Bible study, and no prayer at my house. We only heard about Jesus once a week, so there was no spiritual growth in my life as a kid, but I kept praising God.

When I was a child, I didn't know God had chosen me for such a time as this, and every Sunday was preparing me for right now and what is yet to come. As the years went by, I started serving on the usher board. I was being trained up in the way a child should go. I praise and thank God for teaching me and showing me who I am and who I belong to.

It doesn't matter your age when God calls you and He has need for you; answer His call! God and the Holy Spirit will teach you everything you need to know. Seek God for wisdom, direction, and knowledge. I had to learn from the Holy Spirit and listen to other pastors' sermons about being filled with the Holy Spirit because that teaching was not happening as much in some churches. But I continued to grow in the Lord, and I learned of him. I learned to praise him and honor him in all that I do.

Now that I have received the power and learned of the power of God, I can operate in the kingdom of God. I can let God's purpose and promises come forth in my life. See, we must learn to let God have His way and let His will be done in our lives. We do that by knowing that his will is perfect for our life.

I now know that I am God's wonderful, chosen woman and called by God to do greater works on Earth for His kingdom. I am a woman who God has anointed to pray and lay hands on the sick and to speak life to every dead situation. I am a woman full of faith who carries the gospel of the good news. I am fearless, bold, and courageous, and filled with the Holy Spirit equipped for every good work and trained for every battle. I know that the mighty hand of God is upon my life and his favor surrounds me like a shield. See how I just spoke over myself and what God's word says about me? You should do the same for your life. When times get tough, God's word will forever stand and keep you going. Remember to tell yourself that good news.

2

REBELLIOUS YEARS

For He shall give His angels charge over you, to keep you in all your ways. Psalm 91:11

For many people, those years between being a teen and growing into an adult can be filled with opportunities to stray away from God. Now as an adult I understand the scripture "train a child in the way they should go so in the latter days they won't go astray". When we get to a certain age, we want to do everything that crosses our minds, and we forget about God. But thankfully, God doesn't forget about us, and He keeps His hand on us even when you are doing your own thing. God's hand is protecting you and keeping you from the adversary. Like the scripture says, God will give his angels charge over you and keep you in all your ways.

Sometimes I sit and think that life is like a game of Checkers or chess—God against the devil and our life events are the pieces. It is like God made the first move by creating you in his image. Then the devil tries to destroy that image and discredit our likeness of Him by challenging the word that was spoken over your life. He sees God has chosen me and called me out. Now, he wants to challenge God and try to snatch me out of His hand. But the devil is already defeated, and he knows he can't pluck me out of the hand of God, but it doesn't stop him from trying.

The devil will entice you with all kinds of things that look and feel pleasing to the flesh. He knows what you like and want. When we are young, we think we know everything, and we do not like to listen to guidance. Sometimes our decision making can be tainted by the influences around us. We must be mindful of the company we keep. God's word says, "Be not deceived, evil communications corrupt good manners."

One thing I learned over the years is that the devil is crafty and knows what can tempt you. He is not going to put anything in front of you if you don't already have some desire for it. He will use that same generational curse on you that he used on your ancestors. What your grandmother and your mother experienced, the devil will use to attack you. Be aware of generational curses in your family. It can be anything such as partying, drinking, smoking, mental health or health issues, excessive worrying, teenage pregnancy, single-parent households, lying, molestation, and so on. Those are just some of the generational curses that the devil will attach to our lives.

As I grew up, some of my family's generational curses became clear in my life. They made my life harder and the process to God longer. I started drinking when I was twelve or thirteen years old. My friends and I would get liquor from the corner store or our parents' stashes and go somewhere and get drunk. We would drink during school hours, on school premises. On weekends, we'd drink all day and then go to a club for teens and young adults. In my junior year of high school, I met some true friends who are still my sisters to this day. We stayed over at one another's houses every weekend and sometimes went to school from there. We did this all through high school until we graduated. Our mothers used to get mad at us because we were constantly on the move, running in and out of the house all the time. We would go to school games, parties, and hang out in the neighborhood.

Drinking and hanging out led to other things. Like many people, I met a young man in junior high, and we had a puppy love thing going on straight into high school. We did everything our teenage minds and hormones led us to do. We were young and in love and I was of the mindset that "can't nobody tell me nothing about my teenage love!" That kind of love will have you lied to your parents just to be able to spend time with that person. And boy, I was no different! All of that lying and sneaking around cost me my virginity before I was ready. That took our relationship to another level and made me feel as if I couldn't live without him, and he felt the same. It felt nice and seemed right at the time. We had just created a soul tie that, if left unchecked, could follow us for the rest of our lives. Those types of soul ties hold us back from our true growth spiritually and emotionally. The same spirit that is in them and what they deal with is now attached to you. You would find yourself starting to act like them and do things just like they do. It is hard to get away from it, but you can do it with God's help.

My friends and I considered ourselves female players and did not care about the young men we were involved with. We did what we wanted to do when we wanted to do it. We were just being promiscuous and rebellious in the streets. Some of you remember how it went back in the day. You and your friends hook up with me and my friends. We thought we were just having fun, not realizing what we do affects us later in life. I am a witness that you do reap what you sow. All that fun and not respecting myself and others came at a price in my later years of life.

I was in a gang called W.G.G.—Westside Gangster Girls. We were a group of female friends with common enemies. We'd hang out at different places that teenagers were able to be at without their parents: movies, stores, playgrounds. We hid weapons outside the buildings of the parties we would attend because when the party was over, we knew we were going to fight. Once outside, we'd grab our weapons and start walking knowing that the other girls would most likely start messing with us first; we were ready for whatever. My friends and I dressed alike so everyone could see who was in our crew. I carried a lock on my belt, but some of my friends had knives, forks, and sticks when it was time to fight.

I remember one time I snatched my belt off and cocked it back to hit someone with it and hit myself on the back of my ear. I had the biggest knot on my head and the worst headache. I knew then what it felt like to get hit with that lock. (I told you earlier you reap what you sow.) After every fight, we laughed and talked about who did what.

Our parents were so tired of picking us up after fighting all the time. They even had to come to school because we were starting fights there too. They could not wait until we were freshmen in high school because we were all attending different schools. Our parents were relieved that W. G. G. was no more. At the time, we could not see the hurt and disappointment we were causing them. Now that I'm a parent, I understand the frustration parents feel when their child is living a rebellious lifestyle. The Bible says, "Children, obey your parents in the Lord: for this is right. Honor thy father and mother; which is the first commandment with promise; that it may be well with thee, and thou mayest live long on the Earth." This is how we should've lived back in the day, but we didn't. I now know that God is requiring this from us as children, and I am giving my children that same word. God is just and faithful to forgive all your sins.

Still to this day, from time to time, when we all see one another, we laugh and talk about those days. Like I said before, God is faithful and just. He causes all things to work together for your good! Me and those same girls who we called ourselves W.G.G. back in the day were gangsters in the streets. Now we are all gangsters for the kingdom; we all are ministers or some kind of servants for God. It doesn't matter how you start out; it's how you finish.

I began selling marijuana when I was a sophomore in high school. I took my first paycheck from Taco Bell and bought my first half ounce with it. I was trying to get money. My mother was a single mother working two or three jobs to make ends meet. So, I worked, and I hustled to get what I wanted. As an athlete in school, there are things you must pay for to stay on the team. I also wanted the latest clothes, shoes, and my hair done along with all the other stuff you want as a teenager. I did this throughout my sophomore and junior years of high school.

When it came to my senior year, I missed so many days and credits I couldn't play sports anymore. I was so hurt and mad because I really wanted to play, and your senior year is the best time to shine. I couldn't be mad at anybody but myself. I chose to sell drugs, hang out all night, and miss school. I didn't get to play sports; however, I did graduate on time. I was able to walk with my class and receive my diploma.

See how my past decisions affected my future? That is why you must be wise in your choices even as a child. Young people listen to wise counsel that is around you so you will not make the same mistakes or do something worse. Because what you do might not affect you at that moment, but it will affect you. Trust me. But God still had a plan for my life.

I know firsthand that God will keep you even if you don't want to be kept. God kept me from fatal diseases while I was out there fornicating and living life carelessly while I was believing that I was having a grand old time; not knowing I was really killing my future and picking up negative soul ties along the way. I had been exposing myself to bad habits and bad spirits by being around other people who were just as careless as me, carrying these habits and spirits within me that would manifest when least expected. Occasionally, I stopped to ask myself why I was doing this to myself. But it was a fleeting thought. Looking back, I can recognize just how faithful God really was. He delivered me and many of the people I ran with from the messes we were making and put us on the straight and narrow.

Even though I graduated from high school, I was no more mature than before; I was still doing what I wanted to do, hanging out in the streets with my homegirls. There was usually someone's house we would all hang out at, listening to Mary J. Blige, gossiping, and talking about our problems. One thing about this crew, we were always there for one another. At the time, we were all young single mothers and understood the challenges that we faced trying to make it in this world. Despite the fun we had throughout our young adulthood, we still struggled. I've gone through so much with these girls, I still call them my big sisters. We were products of our environment in so many ways, hanging out in the wrong places with the wrong people. I put myself in dangerous situations that gave the enemy opportunities to corrupt me. The devil tried so many times to take hold of me, but through it all, God said, "she's mine."

I think back to one time my friends and I were at a party. The music was bumping; we were all dancing with boys having fun. Out of nowhere, shots pop off. I hear "get down!" Some people were outside in front of the house shooting, triggering others to start shooting inside the party. God spared us that night, protecting me and my friends—we all walked away without a scratch. That wasn't the only time that God covered us.

Another time, we were leaving the club and one of our male friends was driving us home. He was high or drunk, or both. Suddenly he announced that he was going to kill us all. Pressing his foot on the pedal as far as it could go, the car sped up, flying through all the red lights on that stretch of road. Moving through one of the intersections, I could see bright lights out of the corner of my eye heading right towards us. I held my breath knowing that that car was about to ram into the door that I was next to. But God had other plans. That car missed us by a hair. Thankfully, God saw a reason to keep us from colliding covering us with his angels. I know that God is a keeper, and he will keep you even when you don't want to be kept.

I remember when I used to sell drugs in my early twenties. I was the first one out on the block in the morning and the last one out at night. My supply came easily, and each sale was effortless. I thought it was crazy, but every man I hooked up with sold drugs, so I got my supply at a discount or even for free. Sometimes, guys would buy marijuana just so that they could see me. None of what I was doing then mattered to me, I just wanted the money. I didn't realize back then that the enemy was trying to trap me in that life. The money was good, and things were going well, but it came with a cost.

By this time, I was living on my own, away from my family. Every house I lived in became a "trap house," which is a house where drugs are sold. It's usually the most rundown house on the block where people are constantly coming and going. One day I was sitting in the house and heard a knock at the door. I got up off the couch and opened the door to four young men I knew from around the way. They came in, asked for what they wanted, got it, and left out the back door. After I was back inside on the couch chilling, I thought to myself that they could have come in here and robbed and killed me. It sent a chill up my spine thinking that my family would have been devastated, never knowing what happened to me, but praise be to God.

Fear and the loss of money also kept me stuck in that bad place. Now I know that none of it was worth staying in an abusive relationship. God does not want us to be anyone's step stool. Know your worth and who you are and who you belong to! We are fearfully and wonderfully made children of God. Know it and walk in it. Do not allow anybody to tell you differently or treat you as less than who you know you are.

You are more than enough. If they can't see your worth, God has someone for you who can.

I got out and was on my own. I was living my life. I had my own money, a car, and a house. I thought I had it going on until I got pregnant with my first child. I was twenty-five years old and realized that I could not keep selling drugs because I had a baby to take care of. I wanted this child to be in a safe and loving environment and away from this mess. I had a plan, and it all made sense in my mind, but I didn't stop selling drugs until my baby was about three years old. I would drop him off at my mom's house or she would come over to our house and babysit him while I would be hanging out all day making deals and transactions. I can admit now that I was not attending to my son as a mother should. Even though I was still running the streets, I was feeling the conviction in my spirit about what I was doing. Those thoughts, as well as others, were weighing heavy on me.

That day I asked God to take those thoughts from me. Next thing I knew there was a "drought" that hit our city. I could not find any marijuana anywhere. I knew right then that God was answering my prayers. Even though I was not financially where I wanted to be in the game before I got out, I knew it was time to leave it behind. I did just that.

I worked odd jobs to support myself and my son and left

the street life to the father of my son (we'll call him Dan). He had three other kids by another woman that he had to take care of as well. I considered those babies mine too and most of the time we got along back then. There were times when their mother and I had our disagreements, but we worked it out. I enrolled at Indiana Business College for an accounting degree and graduated with an Associates of Accounting degree in 2002. Life was good. Then things started to change in my relationship with Dan. With all that money and drugs came ghetto fame, and it also attracted the wrong people. Dan cheated on me on such a regular basis that it felt normal. We argued constantly and fought over everything, from bills, to his other kids, to the clothes I wore. One day, God let me know that Dan wasn't for me, and I needed to let him go. Holding on to things that do not serve your highest good will delay the life that God has for you. I thank God every day for discernment.

When I look back now, I truly believe it was necessary for me to go through all that drama, pain, and disrespect. I question myself sometimes and wonder if I had not gone through hardship, would I even know God the way that I do now? Would I trust Him the way that I do? The answer is no! Because to know God on a certain level you must experience God on that level. You can't testify about something you never experienced. I thank God for allowing me to experience such things because now I know God to be a keeper and a way-maker in my life.

I know it's hard to understand sometimes, especially when the struggle or hardship shakes your faith, but I truly believe that it all works together for your good. Because that season you experienced or just came out of was preparing you for your next season. It needs you to show up wiser, stronger, and more faithful than ever before. I know it's easy to get down on yourself or to feel shame for what you have gone through, but if you can hold on to God's unshaking promise and trust the process and what you learn from it, you will be ready to walk into your next season with a testimony!

3

NOT MY BABY! WHY MY BABY? THANK GOD FOR MY BABY!

There hath no temptation taken hold of you but such as is common to man. But God is faithful; He will not suffer you to be tempted beyond that ye are able to bear, but with the temptation will also make a way to escape, that ye may be able to bear.
1 Corinthians 10:13

This next chapter of my journey took my prayer life to a deeper level. My faith, hope, and confidence in God increased in a way that I had never known before. I came to understand that He was the only one who could get me through this, and I was dependent totally on Him for everything. I saw firsthand that God won't put more on me than what I could bear. While I was trusting in God, God was trusting in me to complete His will even when I felt it was too much to handle. He trusts you just the same.

One day, the Holy Spirit came to me and told me that I was going to have another child. When I told a few people in my life, they thought I was crazy. It seemed strange to the few people I told at the time ... crazy that God would do something like that. But God is good and His ways are not our ways, and his thoughts are not our thoughts. God does the unthinkable to advance His kingdom. Because I wasn't married that meant that I had to fornicate. That seems like it is going against His word, but God says all things work together for your good. God can even use your sin that you are already in. He will turn it around and cause it to work for you and bring you out of that sin.

This time of my life reminded me of the story of Mary, Jesus's mother. An angel of the Lord came to her and told her she was pregnant, and the child she was carrying would rule and save the people. Never in a million years would I have thought that God would use me or my situation to advance His kingdom on Earth. Yet, God did. And it was time for God's will to be done. So, take it from me that no matter the situation you are going through, God's plan will come forth. Never think that He can't use you and your mess for His will to be done. He can make what the enemy meant for evil to work out for your good.

Let God use you and trust the process!

When I heard that word from the Holy Spirit, I did not receive it. I didn't want another baby. I wasn't married, and I was just trying to live my best life. I thought about all the worries all parents think of—another baby would cost more money, getting a babysitter for one child was hard enough, etc. On top of that, Dan and I were not doing well in our relationship, and I was scared I'd have to raise another child by myself. If it was up to me, I would have waited to have another baby, but God's will shall be done, no matter what.

I wrestled with God about having another baby. God was saying yes, and I was saying no. This went on every day for a month. I didn't have any peace within me. I couldn't sleep at night and was barely eating. This was constantly on my mind. I could not shake it off. I even had dreams about being pregnant. God kept talking to me about having a baby. I kept saying no to God and I tried to block it from my mind. Foolishly, I thought I could escape the will of God. That feeling is like running from someone or hiding something and it is constantly on your mind. It's that feeling you get in your stomach when God tells you to go right, and you go left.

One day in November I had enough of carrying this burden around in my mind and doing what I thought was disobeying God. I worked all day thinking and feeling conflicted about having this baby that by the time I got home I just screamed and said, "Okay, I will do it!" I finally submitted to God's will and gave up my own. There is no peace within until you allow the will of God. He will not let you rest until you submit to his will and purpose. But once I said yes to his will, there was an indescribable peace I felt; a peace that surpasses all understanding. Now the will of God can go forth because you come to an agreement with his plan.

I felt like Mary in more ways than one. The spirit told her she would give birth to a son who would save the world. That same spirit came to me and said I would have another baby. What I didn't know at that time was that my baby, Keyon, would come to save my life from this world. One thing I know is that you can't run from the will of God. God will cause you to submit and do what He is calling you to do for His kingdom. Your situation is never about you; it is all about God's purpose. God knows how to get you back on track and in alignment with his will even when you are going down the wrong path. He knows how to get your attention. For he knows the heart and intentions of man, so he knows what to do to change your heart and turn it towards him.

I am trusting God because He knew me before I entered my mother's womb. God knew what to place on my path to change me and prepare me for such a time as this. God has a plan for you too. God sometimes needs to interrupt your path to get you on to His path. He will allow or send something to happen that looks and feels like a tragedy or setback, but he turns it into triumph. When you see the situation or person through the eyes of God, you will be praising and thanking Him. God uses these situations to draw you closer to him and to get you on the path of his will and righteousness.

God allows the situation to be so bad that can't nobody fix it but Him. He is our very present help in the time of trouble. God, Abba, the Father, is all you need to get you through. He will show you how to get through it and be right there with you the whole time so you will not fail or give up. I know all about this because he was there with me through all my tough times. God brought me out of every one of them better, more faithful, and victorious. That is why now I say it was good that I was afflicted. God took my mess and made it into a masterpiece.

Even your sin God can use to make you win!

Your sinful life may look like a mess to you and everyone around you, but God sees an opportunity to show himself mighty and strong. I know some of y'all are thinking that God did not come to me and tell me that I was going to have another baby with a man I wasn't even married to, but He did just that. I am a witness that He will use any situation to advance his kingdom. God did it through me.

About a month after I surrendered, I was pregnant. I still held on to a little bit of anger, but I knew it was going to happen. Day to day my feelings changed. One day I was on board, another day I considered having an abortion. Life was challenging, and I was struggling financially so that made me have a rough time seeing myself through this new pregnancy. Even after I heard the word from God and saw it come to pass, the enemy was putting confusion and doubt in my mind.

The enemy didn't stop there either. Fear and frustration were being cultivated in my spirit making me toy with the idea of throwing in the towel and giving up on God. Looking back now, I think I had trouble accepting His will because it was not what I wanted for my life. But God's ways of doing things are not like our ways nor are his thoughts like our thoughts. I had to keep in mind, "Not my will but God's will be done."

The idea of having an abortion came up more than once and this one day, I kept coming up with reasons to do it. I even tried to justify it by saying that I already had a son and hoped for a daughter instead. But God had a solution for every concern I had. That same night I had a dream. God opened my womb and showed me three children. The first was a crying baby girl. She was the closest to my belly button. That shocked me the most and I jumped up out of my sleep excited about having a girl. That's when the whole idea of an abortion went out the door because I thought I was having a girl. Next, I saw a little boy in a blue onesie crawling. Lastly, I saw a kid standing in the background.

Dreams are not always what they seem. You can interpret your dreams wrong if God does not give you a revelation. I interpreted my dream wrong, and I didn't ask God for a revelation of what I dreamed. Not once did I ask God what that dream meant, nor did I ask him to reveal it to me.

I gave birth to three kids just like in the dream, but I misinterpreted the order of their births. I thought the first child I saw was the one I was carrying but now I know she was the last child I would bring into the world, my daughter, Kimmyah. And the child I saw standing in the background was my first son Keymonie. Keyon, my second child, was the toddler crawling in the blue onesie.

The enemy hates to see a person's purpose fulfilled, so he kept my head filled with thoughts of abortion—and I entertained the thought knowing that God would forgive me if I asked. The enemy kept whispering "go ahead and get the abortion." Just like he tricked Eve in the Garden by sowing the seed of discord in her life saying you won't die if you eat from the tree of life. See, he only told part of the truth because you will die spiritually and relationally with God.

My God is so awesome with how he does things in our lives. God knew I was going to choose his plan that's why he showed it to me. Let me make this clear; I in no way feel that God tricked me into doing His will. I just perceived the dream wrong. I only saw what I wanted to see and that was the little girl. I didn't seek God for clarity and that was on me. Because if I had asked, he would have made it clear for me. He knew I would misinterpret the dream and that would make me want to keep the baby. That is why all things work together for your good, even when you are wrong. God can do and use anything to advance His kingdom. Trust in Him.

In many situations, we find ourselves leaning on our own understanding instead of going to God and acknowledging him. For he is the one who will direct the path. If I would have gone to God as soon as I woke up and asked him to interpret that dream for me, He would have led me in the right direction. Don't get discouraged if you make the wrong choice, say the wrong thing, or even choose the wrong path because God is all-knowing. God already knows what you are going to do, say, and think before you even do it. That is why God provides a way for you to escape the snare.

God showed me that dream so that I could escape the foolish thinking that was keeping me captive. I praise and thank him for His omniscience. There is none like him!

While writing this book, I stopped many times thinking over my life and how God is a keeper, my keeper. I can't help but give praise. Take a moment and have a praise break too. When I think about the goodness of God and all He is to me and all he has done for me, I can't help but say Hallelujah!! It is hard to keep your composure when you think about where God has brought you from.

This second pregnancy was different from my first one. I had morning sickness and sometimes pain in my abdomen. Since this pregnancy was not going like the first one, I thought maybe it was because I was carrying a girl. During the entire first trimester all I could think about was my future daughter. There I was again leaning on my own understanding instead of seeking God. Sometimes we do that because we want what we want, and we think it is God's will for our lives.

During my fourth month of pregnancy, it was time for an ultrasound. I was excited about going to see the doctor because she was going to be telling me what we were having. My children's father didn't care one way or another, but I was still hoping for a girl. I was excited and eager to know what the doctor had to say. My doctor checked everything, and all was well, everything looked good. She asked if I wanted to know the sex of the baby, excitedly I said yes. She turned the monitor towards me while I was still laying down and said, "It's a boy!" I can admit that I was disappointed. I had the nerve to say aloud, "Another boy! I thought you said I was having a girl!" I was still believing that God had made a mistake as if I had some control over His purpose for my life. Now I look back and laugh at the foolish things I said and did! God never said anything like that. I wanted what I wanted, and I misperceived my dream.

Often time this is what we do: we put the blame on God or someone else when we don't get the outcome we want. But if I had acknowledged Him first as soon as I woke up from that dream, I might not have been disappointed. I learned a lot from that experience. When I dream now, I know to first acknowledge God. Then ask him what it is that I should be gleaning from it and what to do with that information. Don't try to figure it out on your own because that could lead to disappointment or setbacks.

God will use every moment of your life for his Glory. He chose to use this baby and pregnancy for the kingdom of God. Throughout my pregnancy I was reading the word of God and praying more than ever before, drawing closer to Him. Up to that point, there were no complications, and everything was going well. God is all knowing and was preparing me for what was yet to come. He was equipping me with His words, and they were increasing my faith in Him daily. I grew to know God on a different level.

One day at church service, a lady prophesied to me that there would be travail in this pregnancy and some problems with the baby, but all was going to be well. She did not go into detail, and I was too taken aback to ask her more about it. I had all kinds of thoughts and fears, but I prayed to God about it and felt a peace over me. I didn't worry about it anymore after that.

The time had come for my baby to be born. I had a scheduled C-section because my first pregnancy was an emergency C-Section. The doctor said that it was safer to deliver your other babies the same way as the first. Thankfully, the delivery was a success! He was here—an eight-pound, twenty-one-inch beautiful baby boy. We already had a name for him: Keyon William Allen. I was immediately in love with him! He had a light brown complexion and a head full of slick black hair. He was just perfect to me.

The nurses let me see him for a minute before they took him and cleaned him up. They noticed that Keyon was having complications breathing. When they tried to feed him from the bottle, he would inhale the milk. The doctor called it aspiration. Another thing the doctor noticed right away was his arm. No matter how we tried to put it down it would flop right back to his chest.

Since Keyon was having complications, he could not go home with me on our release date and had to stay an extra couple of days. Upon his release, he was given a feeding tube through his nose to help him get the nourishment that babies need.

His father and I had to learn how to properly place the tube through his nose before he could go home. That was not an easy thing to do as a mother. I thought I was hurting him, and it was painful to watch him squirm. You also have feelings of not wanting to see your baby go through something like that. But God gives you the strength to go through whatever you are facing in that moment. I had to learn to trust God and allow him to lead and guide me through this process.

I asked God to guide my hands and deepen my understanding on how to properly care for my son. This type of care needed more of my focus and time because once I have gotten the tube through his nose, I needed to pump air into it and listen to his belly with a stethoscope to make sure it was in the right spot. Then I had to give him a small amount of food at a time. Then I had to wait about a minute to let that first amount settles and then pour another small amount in the tube. That was the only way to feed Keyon.

Then it was time for his one-week checkup, and Keyon was not responding to the reflex tests that the doctors perform on newborns. His doctor was not satisfied with his performance and told me to bring him back the following week because he thought Keyon was just being lazy. That next week it was time for another doctor's appointment, and Keyon still did not pass the reflex tests. The doctor called in another doctor and when she was checking him out the look on her face said it all. Her eyebrows raised and she could barely look me in the eyes. She said, "I had just seen a baby with something like this."

I will never forget those words. Both doctors left the room, and when they came back, they had nurses and other doctors with them. Next thing I knew, the main doctor said they wanted to admit Keyon so they could run more tests on him.

Keyon was admitted into the hospital about the third week of October 2004. He stayed there for two months, and I visited every day and sat with him all day. I did not know what to do except pray for my baby. My heart ached every time I went to see him in the hospital. I cried while I was there and all the way back home. Each time I left the hospital I left a piece of my heart with Keyon. By the time I got home from those visits I settled myself down, trying to be strong for everyone at home. I still had my oldest son to take care of, and I didn't want him or anyone else to see me break down. My mom would come over and take care of Keymonie while I was with Keyon. Whenever she asked how Keyon was doing, I'd answer, "He's okay," while fighting back tears. This was my routine for several weeks.

I remember one day, after running several blood tests on him, the doctors finally found out what was wrong. They called Dan and me into a room full of doctors, nurses, social workers, and nursing home providers. Seeing all these people in one room really scared and overwhelmed me. I could feel how serious this was. The doctors told us that Keyon had a rare genetic disease called Spinal Muscular Atrophy (SMA). SMA is a disorder that affects breathing, muscle weakness, spine, and even swallowing, which explains the feeding tube. Basically, the body's muscles don't respond to signals from the brain, so they get weak and shrink.

There are four different types of SMA, and doctors determine which type you have by the age it was detected in you. Keyon had type 1, which has a life expectancy of two years. Keyon's symptoms started at birth just like most children who have type 1. The signs of type 1 SMA are trouble breathing, swallowing while feeding, limited movement, and being unable to sit or stand without support. Remember I said when Keyon was born, he had trouble breathing and eating and his arm was stuck to his chest? All those were signs that my baby had SMA. This disease was very rare back in 2004 so there was little education about it, not like it is now. But even today there is still no cure for SMA. Researchers are doing a lot of research to find ways to slow down progression.

That day in the hospital room really shook me to my core. Even with all those different doctors and specialists telling me and Dan all that they knew about this disease, all I could think about was sitting and talking to our Father in heaven and how he was going to heal Keyon. I couldn't wait to talk to God about this! Before I was pregnant with Keyon, God had me study in the Bible the book of John. God showed me all these miracles that Jesus was performing on Earth. It caused me to believe in God's word and miracles. He will prepare you for whatever you are about to face, or should I say what is about to face you when you are a child of God and full of faith. God was showing me how he can heal, deliver, and set us free, which increased my faith in Him and what he can do for Keyon. I couldn't wait to get out of that room to put my petition before God because I knew he was the only one who could handle this situation with my baby.

In the hospital room that day, they had the nerve to have some nursing home faculty there, like I was going to let my baby go to a nursing home. They thought his dad and I were too young to take care of a child with this type of medical condition. They didn't know that I serve a god who can do anything but fail, and they didn't understand my level of faith. I believe that I can do all things through Christ who strengthens me! I told those doctors and nurses to teach me everything I need to know to take care of my baby.

Dan and I had to complete so many hours of nursing to bring him home with us. We also needed another person as a backup caregiver to also learn how to care for him. I asked my mom if she would be that person, but she said that she couldn't stand to keep seeing him like that. It really hurt that I couldn't count on her. But God had a ram in the bush. He was preparing one of my aunts to step in.

At the time, my aunt Sheila was working at Methodist Hospital, and she would visit him on her lunch breaks. On one of her visits, I asked her if she could be the third caretaker we needed, and she did not hesitate to say yes. This allowed us to finally take Keyon home after four months in the hospital. During that time while Keyon was in the hospital, I remember crying my eyes out every time I had to leave him there. This was affecting me not only emotionally but mentally. I felt worried, stress, and anxiety daily. I found myself struggling with how to deal with this and I also needed strength to take care of my other son because he needed me too. People would try to encourage me and pray for me and help me when they could, but I needed a word from God.

One of those days after leaving the hospital, I could barely put my bags down at home before I broke down in the middle of my living room. I just cried and cried and asked God, "Why Keyon? Why my baby?!" God spoke back. He said, "So that I can heal him." When God spoke those words to me, I was immediately encouraged and my tears dried up. I was able to press on and keep going. My faith was restored because faith comes by hearing the word of God. That was all I needed to keep going because I believed God at His word and nothing else mattered!

It was so difficult seeing my baby day after day lying there unable to help him or take away his illness. But God was giving me strength every day to keep going and take care of my children without losing my mind. He was there from the beginning, and He never left me. The same way that I was there in that hospital room every day for Keyon, God was there for me. I would not have been able to be my baby's strength without Him. When Keyon eventually came home from the hospital, he had a G-tube, a trachea, a ventilator, monitors, and he needed oxygen twenty-four hours a day, seven days a week. Things were kind of tight.

We lived in a two-bedroom house with Keyon and all his supplies and oxygen tanks, and we needed more space. I was in a Section 8 housing program in Indiana. It provides low-income families like mine with affordable housing. But we were denied a three-bedroom house because the boys were too close in age. I was told that they would have to share a room, but Keyon needed his own space.

I'm sure by now you know what I did. I prayed and asked God for a three-bedroom house for me and my boys. As a mother, I will do anything for my kids. I gave up my Section 8 housing assistance, and God opened a door for us to move into a three-bedroom just like I asked for.

This new house was bigger and better than the one before. It was located on the far west side on a nice street where my older son could go outside and safely play. He was able to ride his bike without drug traffic and shootings. Things were coming together. Keyon began receiving nursing services. They came out to the house in the mornings and stayed for hours, giving us a little break during the day. My kids' father was still in the streets making street money to pay the bills and take care of us. I finally felt as if everything was right and that I could breathe a little.

Then, one night I had a dream that scared me. In it, a nurse wearing all white had just given Keyon a bath and he was rolling around on a big white sheet. It was like the nurse was an angel and Keyon was in heaven. In the dream, I repeated, "Come here, Keyon!" But he would not come to me; he just kept rolling around and laughing. He was playing and having fun not listening to anything I was saying. Then I used my "momma" voice on him and said, "Keyon, get over here." Before he could respond, I woke up. That dream had me spooked. I was not ready for my baby to go.

A couple of days had gone by and that same nurse came over to the house to take care of Keyon. She had just gotten done giving him a bath when I heard her call his name several times. It sounded different than usual, so I went to see what was going on. Keyon had stopped breathing. Looking back now, I believe that dream was a warning. God was warning me or more like giving me a heads up to be prepared.

I called 911 while the nurse was doing everything she was trained to do. Dan was also there, crying and pacing back and forth. Unable to control his nerves, he began to vomit. I was still on the phone telling the dispatcher everything that was going on with Keyon. As soon as the medics arrived, they began trying to get my baby to breathe.

I stood there watching, praying, and crying because I couldn't do anything else to help. I was becoming impatient and mad. I was still holding on to what God told me before, that He [Keyon] must have it so that I can heal him. I felt that I needed to remind God of His word that he spoke to me.

I went to my bedroom, shut the door, and fell to my knees. I looked toward heaven and shouted, "God, you didn't say this!"

I believed God at His word, so I was expecting God to heal Keyon but not through death. I was expecting God to heal him on Earth, not in heaven. Even through my closed door, I heard one of the paramedics say, "We have a pulse." I got up off the floor, grabbed my things, and ran out of my bedroom just in time to see them rushing Keyon out to the ambulance. I was right behind them and followed them all the way to the hospital. When I got there, I got the feeling that the doctors seemed to be giving up on Keyon, but I still had my faith and was still standing on God's word.

The doctors said that Keyon's disease only gave him eighteen months to live, and at that time Keyon was almost one year old. If my faith wasn't as strong as it was, I would have believed them. But God! I was praying and crying as the family started to gather at the hospital. The doctors came out to speak with Dan and me letting us know that Keyon lost a lot of brain activity because he was without oxygen too long. They told us that they didn't think that he would make it through the night. But I had faith in God! I knew my baby was going to make it.

Riley Hospital for Children was such a blessing to our family. They set up a room for us at the Ronald McDonald House so that we could be close to Keyon if anything happens throughout the night. Ronald McDonald House is like a hotel for parents to stay close to their children while they are in the hospital. There was a kitchen to cook in and a lounge area for parents to gather and get to know one another. I stayed in the room all night praying and reading the word of God. My faith was strong, and I just knew Keyon would be coming home with us soon. God is faithful and honored my faith. Thankfully, Keyon pulled through the night and was able to go home a couple of days later.

Before Keyon was released from the hospital, the doctors told us that he was not going to get better, and they were just going to make him comfortable while he is here on Earth. Basically, they were saying it's all downhill from there. His brain was without oxygen for too long and the lack of brain activity could not be reversed, but I still believed in God.

I was sure that it was reversible, and I told the doctor that she was wrong and needed to find a way to help him. I was so mad at the staff and how they were talking to us. I could have hit the doctor on the head so that she could see how it felt. But nevertheless, I remained calm and went to talk to Abba

Father, about it.

When Keyon was released from the hospital, he continued with his physical therapy. He was able to wave his hand hi and bye, smile, and move his eyes with intention. That was the only movement Keyon had. But as the years went by, Keyon lost movement in his hand, and he lost his smile. I remained in prayer and God remained faithful in keeping my son.

A couple of years went by and Keyon was doing fine. We celebrated his birthday every year with a big party full of friends and family. Dan and I had split up by that point. The bills were not getting paid. It was time for me to go back to work, so I started a part-time job. I had to get comfortable with leaving Keyon at home, and then I began to work full time. Even though money was tight, I witnessed God take care of me and my kids. Every bill was paid and all our needs were met according to God's riches in glory.

In 2007, God intervened in my life and changed it for the better. Even though it felt like I was dying inside, I knew this was a life-changing event that was ordained by God. I had been praying for a husband and a new house. I met a man who wanted to get married and build a life with me and my boys. I prayed for direction from God about this move and this man. And so, it was! God granted us a new place to live, once again.

Even though I prayed for it, when it was moving time, I

cried like a baby because it felt as if I was leaving so much behind. I had lived out west, but God moved us to the east side of town. It was something new for me, but God had a plan, and I thank him for it now. The man I was dating never moved in, and we split up once the boys, and I were settled in the house. God used him to pay for the house and for us to have a new start. I believe that was that man's purpose in my life. Even to this day, I haven't seen him or heard from him since then.

Keyon, Keymonie, and I were living in this big, beautiful house in the east and things were fine. Keyon was doing well too, and I continued to work full time. It was hard taking care of the household and two kids, but God provided. From the outside, things were running relatively smoothly, but many days and nights, after the boys had gone to bed, I cried out to God for strength to keep going. I took Keyon to church every Sunday. I'd pack up his oxygen tanks, ventilator, the suction machine, and a diaper bag to go anywhere with him. My oldest son Keymonie was still very young, but he was a big help to me. I was tired and worn out some days, but God gave me strength to keep going. I prayed and prayed for Keyon's healing year after year. And God gave me grace year after year to keep enduring. I praised God for his grace every day because it was only through him that I was able to continue with raising my boys and staying sane.

On Christmas day, I noticed that Keyon was bleeding from his rectum. I rushed him to the hospital that morning and he was diagnosed with ulcerative colitis, so we spent our Christmas in the hospital. My oldest son was with his dad so that he could have an enjoyable holiday. This new diagnosis weighed heavy on me, but I know God doesn't make mistakes. He knows what He is doing in my life. My God is still worthy of praise.

At this time, Keyon was going home with more medications than ever before and another illness for us to treat. He was getting his regular care daily, and I was working, taking care of the boys, and trusting God through it all. God was shining on us every day.

In the middle of 2007, I met my future husband at a gas station of all places. My son and I were on the way home from his school and we needed gas. We approached a stop light and a gas station on my left. Normally I would pass this gas station because it was always crowded, and I didn't like to go there. But it seemed like my car was pulled in the direction of that gas station and when we pulled up to the pump, I noticed a man looking at me. I told myself that if he spoke to me, I would be mean to him so that he would leave me alone. I walked inside to pay the cashier and sure enough, while I walked back to my car, that same man came over to talk to me. He was kind and charming and surprisingly, so was I. We exchanged numbers and began dating right away.

Two years later in November we got married. This man accepted me and my boys. He even learned how to take care of Keyon. In October 2010 we had a daughter, and she was everything I prayed for. I had wanted a girl ever since I could remember. I really looked forward to dressing her up and doing mommy and daughter things. However, she had different plans. As a baby, she was a total daddy's girl. Nevertheless, things were good. My husband and I had our share of normal marital problems, but God saw us through them all.

I spent many days and nights praying and crying out to God for my family and specifically for Keyon's healing. Each time I prayed I wondered when the change was going to come. I called on Jehovah Rapha (God thy healer) because I knew he was the only one who could heal my son. Friends, family, and even church members all tried to encourage me. They would say things like, "You know, God can heal him on the other side." That sentiment always bothered me. I believed God to heal him on Earth just like He showed me in His word. People were being healed from all kinds of illnesses and diseases. I believed God did it for them and he would do it for Keyon too. I know there is nothing too hard for God; He is a miracle worker. I was totally convinced that God can and would heal Keyon on Earth and all men would marvel at the sight of His work.

I'd sit and daydream about testifying on how God healed Keyon and how He has been good to us. My face was set like a flint. I did not waver on Keyon's healing. I believed God for it, and I knew God was going to do it. It was just a matter of time. Waiting for Keyon's healing was not easy, but I stood firm on it, and I was willing to do whatever I needed to do for my baby. Fasting and praying became my way of life.

I had many sleepless nights worrying about my baby boy as well as giving him the care he needed. Keyon required medical attention every two hours for about a year and then it went to every four hours of the day. This felt like progress. I relied on God to wake me up on time and to keep me alert for anything Keyon needed, and God was faithful every time. Anytime Keyon needed suctioning, a trachea changed, his G-tube cleaned, or to move into a new position, God made me aware. I would get a feeling that I needed to check on him, and I knew it was the Holy Spirit operating through me.

Only with a relationship with God are we able to discern what He is telling us; He will direct you to where you need to be at the right time. He sends a comforter to help, lead, and guide us throughout this life. He sent the Holy Spirit to soothe and help in all things. I knew I was not alone in this and that I had supernatural help.

As the years went by it started taking a toll on me. I began having back pains due to lifting and carrying Keyon up and down the stairs with his ventilator and oxygen tank. Although he was small for his size, he was getting bigger and heavier and nothing got easier, but God was helping me. People don't know how many days and nights I struggled to take care of my baby boy, but God was there every step of the way. When it was time to lift him, I would say, "Come on God, help me." And he would be right there helping me lift my child. God is a very present help not just in trouble, but when you need him from day to day.

All you need to do is call on him!

In addition to church, I also took Keyon to doctor visits and family gatherings. At least once or twice a week I'd pack up the car with his wheelchair, suction machine, ventilator, heart monitor, two oxygen tanks, and a bag. I know it seems like a lot, and you're probably wondering why we just didn't stay home. Of course that would have been easy, but I love Keyon the same way I love my other kids and wanted him to experience as much of life as he could. My family would accommodate us in their homes and at church. That in and of itself was a blessing.

There were plenty of times during these days that I'd have a breakdown because I was overwhelmed. Sometimes, when I was in a room alone, I'd drop to the floor and just cry asking God, "Why my baby? When are you going to heal my baby? God, please help my baby!" It was still very tough seeing Keyon go through all the things he had to go through each day. He needed assistance with everything—he couldn't do anything for himself. He couldn't even let me know if something was itching or if something was hurting him. All he was able to do was hope that I'd rub the right spot or move him to a more comfortable position.

Seeing my baby having to go through all that gave me a different outlook on life and how we sometimes take things for granted. We really don't understand how privileged we are. That fact that we can do what we can do is only by God's grace because at any given time anything could happen that might change your life. Going through something like this will humble you and cause you to walk in the spirit of humility. It will cause you to appreciate the small things in life.

Keyon had a humble spirit. He rarely cried even in all that he was going through. He'd often just lay there watching tv and never mumble a word. He had peace that surpassed all understanding. When he did cry, it was because something was hurting him or he was uncomfortable, but for the most part he didn't complain. God will give you grace to go through a hard time in your life.

Keyon was teaching me so much. There'd be days I'd walk into his room feeling upset about something and then I'd see his machines and remember how much he endures just to live. Once I'd see him, I'd forget all about the little things that really didn't matter. Keyon has helped me to see life in a new way and to see people in a better light. This experience has taught me to have more of the fruits of the Spirit. I have patience and understanding now for people who are long suffering; most of all I learned not to complain. I learned to take everything to God in prayer. I had many long prayer days and nights, fasting, sowing seeds, and praying for Keyon's healing.

Years have gone by with ups and downs with Keyon's health, but I never stopped believing in God for his healing. Doctors had given up on him years ago, but I didn't. Even when I didn't see an improvement in his health, I kept believing and trusting God through this journey.

God remained faithful through it all.

It's now 2012, and my baby Keyon was seven years old. That was reason enough for a praise break! Remember, the doctors only gave Keyon eighteen months to live because of SMA. What a mighty God we serve! He is a keeper and a way-maker! I remember one day that summer when I was driving home from work and praying. I will never forget that prayer. I said, "God, you got to heal Keyon because it is time for me to be about your business." I remember this prayer like it was yesterday. Those words seemed to unlock something or gave God the go-ahead to do what He was going to do because I was now ready.

That September, Keyon was admitted to the hospital for pneumonia. He gets pneumonia occasionally because of his condition, so I wasn't too worried. Usually when he was in the hospital, I'd stay overnight with him, but this Sunday I went to see him after church. A nurse on duty told me that I should go home and get some rest because they could take care of my baby, and they would call me if they needed to. The nurse had me thinking that this would be a routine visit and that I should take advantage of getting some sleep or cleaning the house. Thinking back now, maybe Keyon's hospital visits were God's way of giving me some rest.

During this visit, after talking to the nurse on duty, when I walked into Keyon's room it seemed like a light was shining on him because his face was glowing. I ran in there and touched the side of his face with my hand and kissed him on the cheek, rubbing my cheek against his as I did often. I took his hand and rubbed it against my face. That was our way of greeting. He was laying there watching tv, so I sat with him for a while and I was so happy because Keyon looked good, and his face was clear. He was not drooling, and he didn't need suction the whole time I was there. This was cause for praise. I thanked God for his healing. I knew my son was coming home from the hospital. I was so excited I called my sister and told her the good news. We were on the phone praising God together.

The next day, Keyon came home from the hospital. I noticed that he did not need suction like he used to. He wasn't even drooling anymore. My excitement was growing because I could see God's healing over my son. I was ready for him to get up out of that bed and walk.

It was the middle of the week, and everything was running smoothly. I worked, and when I got home the nurse said Keyon didn't need suctioning all that day. I looked at her and laughed, *thinking that's because God is healing Keyon.* I got ready for Bible study and went to church, leaving Keyon with the nurse. When I got back home, she had the same report of Keyon not needing any suctioning while I was gone. She ended her shift, and I got the kids ready for bed before having my devotional time with God and then going to bed myself. God woke me up at four in the morning to hear my son's machine alarm going off. I rushed to his room, and all I could see in the dark room was his eyes looking up toward the ceiling. I said aloud, "I know you aren't dead in here." I turned the light on and started calling his name, but he did not respond. Then I started doing everything the doctors and nurses trained us to do if a situation like this happened. I suctioned him and changed his trachea. Keyon still didn't respond.

Keymonie woke up and came across the hall to Keyon's room asking me what was wrong with his brother. I told him to call 911. When the emergency services arrived, I left the room so that they could work on my son. I told my husband to take our daughter to daycare so that I could stay with Keyon and go to the hospital with him.

I felt the presence of God so strongly holding me, and I kept hearing God whisper in my ear, "Let him go." As I paced up and down the hallway, He was singing to me and kept whispering "Let him go." I peeked into the bedroom every few seconds to see the look on the paramedics' faces. They all looked grim. But in my mind, I could not bring myself to believe what that meant. I think that is why they worked on him for so long. But they finally called it and said there was nothing else they could do and pronounced him dead.

My faith was so strong that I didn't believe them! I also

believed that God could still raise him from the dead. I remembered years ago when God told me that Keyon "must have it" so that He could heal him. So, I believed God for His healing on Earth. I kept his trachea in his throat, and I kept him on the ventilator with oxygen even after they pronounced him dead. I remember someone in the house asking me why I had those machines and devices still on him, and I said that he might need them when he wakes up. I didn't even realize what I said until after I said it. My faith was unmoving! God would have honored it and brought him back to me if I would've asked him. That is why I believe he was holding me so tightly and whispering in my ear to let him go. I had the kind of faith that God would have to honor His word if I would have spoken it out of my mouth.

My spiritual mother came over at that time. My husband saw her at the church when he was dropping our daughter off at daycare and told the intercessors what was going on. They came over after the five-a.m. prayer service. Keyon was still in bed because the funeral home had not picked up his body yet. I was sitting on the floor next to his bed rubbing and holding his hand. My spiritual mother came into the room and got on the floor with me asking me what I wanted to do next.

You need people with faith like yours around you.

Some people have faith, some have water-walking faith, and some have dead-raising faith. Whatever measure of faith God gave you, use it. When she asked me what I wanted to do I couldn't even open my mouth. All I could do was shrug my shoulders. The Lord would not let me speak it out of my mouth. I believe that if I would have spoken it, and with her faith and mine, God would have to bring him back to life.

Nevertheless, God's will be done on Earth as it is in heaven. On September 13, 2012, my baby son Keyon William Allen was called home to be with God. He took his rest from battling with SMA. That night I cried and asked God to let me hold him one more time. I wished I had known this was going to happen. I would've stayed home from church and spent the day with him if I knew that was going to be his last day on Earth. God is so kind and loving He allowed me to have a dream that night.

In my dream, Keyon was there in an all-white suit and everything around us was white. I called for Keyon to come to me, but he just laughed and continued to play so carefree. He finally came and I held him and kissed him. I woke up still holding on to him. That dream felt so real! I knew God allowed me to have that time with him just like I asked. I was crying, but it did my heart some good to be able to hold him one more time.

Keyon's funeral was two weeks later. His white suit with its gold buttons matched his casket. His favorite toy sat on top of a bed of flowers on top of his casket. It was perfect! The church was packed; everyone was dressed in white and gold. God even gave me the strength to speak at the front of the church to encourage and remind the people that no matter what you go through or what they say about you, God has the last say so. Doctors said that Keyon was only supposed to live for eighteen months; but God said seven years. It's no coincidence that seven is the number that represents completion and wholeness in the Bible.

Keyon experienced suffering and pain while he was here on Earth. He went through all of that so that I can come through and be who God called me to be. He reminded me of Jesus; he came, lived, suffered, and died for the people to live. Keyon came, lived, suffered, and died for me to live in Christ. His life changed my life. His life caused me to come out of the streets and take care of him. His life drew me closer to God because I had to seek God for everything with Keyon. I needed God's help, and only He could do it.

I believed God to heal him because I read it in His word.

So, when I didn't see the healing that I wanted to see I got discouraged. I'll admit that I was mad at God. I was disappointed *in* God! I didn't understand why he didn't heal Keyon on Earth, especially when I believed him to do so.

I carried those feelings and emotions for some time. I couldn't shake it off because I had faith, and I didn't understand why my prayer went unanswered. After a while, God showed it to me. That Sunday I had a church meeting. While sitting there I broke down crying. God had revealed to one of the ladies at the meeting that I was mad at Him. She prayed for me. I cried out to God asking for forgiveness, and God heard me and delivered me that day.

It took a long time to accept my son being gone. My days were lost. I would cry in the shower every morning for hours. I didn't know what to do with my time because I used to be with Keyon during certain times of the day giving him breathing treatment or whatever else he needed. I'd find myself crying in the car while driving. I was sick to my stomach and felt like I couldn't breathe at times. A piece of my heart was gone, and that void felt unbearable. I felt like a part of me died with Keyon. My heart was beyond broken.

Remember that prayer I told y'all before? God had me release Keyon to do His work by speaking it, and he performed it. Now I am living it, and it all works together for my good.

Because like I said before, *Not my baby! Why my baby? Thank God for my baby!* Those were the three stages I went through for my baby. At first, I couldn't believe it. Then I couldn't understand it. Now I know why because his life changed my life for the better. His life will not be in vain. God's word will be accomplished in my life because Keyon died for me.

During those seven years, God showed me so much. He showed me who He was and who I am in him. You never know the trial or tribulation that God will use to get you to come to him. We must trust God and his process while we are going through it. God knows the plans he has for you; not to harm but to prosper you. Even when it hurts, he still has your best interest at heart. God is the only one who can cause all things to work together for your good. Who would have thought that having a child with a disability could bring me out of the streets and into a covenant with God? Only God can turn a tragedy into a triumph!

4

THE SHAPING AND MOLDING YEARS

But now thus saith the Lord who created thee, O Jacob, and He that formed thee, O Israel: Fear not, for I have redeemed thee; I have caked thee by name; thou art mine.
Isaiah 43:1

When God has called you for His kingdom there is nothing you can do but answer and submit to his will. You will go through so many trials and tribulations it will make you want to give up on God and on life. But you can't give up because it is bigger than you. You are just the vessel God uses to show his glory to the world. Do you know there are things that only you can perform in this world for God? There are people waiting to receive a word from you that will change their life. You go through challenges so that your testimony will inspire others to overcome their own hardships. But how can you testify if you've never been through a test? How can you encourage someone else through their storm?

Think about one of the hardest times in your life; whether it was a sickness or disease, it could be death or divorce, or financial problems. When you received the news, it hurt and you felt helpless. You prayed and turned it over to Him. And when God brought you through it you were able to testify about what He did and how you overcame it all. It makes you better, stronger, wiser, and more equipped for the next challenge.

From each one of my trials, I learned something that will be able to help someone else. These trials are bigger than us and require faith in God knowing that it won't be in vain. Let Him use you! God said all things work together for your good anyway, so you will see the blessing in it one day. I saw the positive at the end of each trial, and I praise God for every one of them. I can now say Thank you Lord! It was purposeful that I was afflicted. It made me better and I felt God on a new level.

God reveals himself during a trial, and you will know Him by that name. You will have the power to call on the name of God. It will mean something different to you than just hearing it from the preacher. You will know him for yourself, and no one can take that away from you! You will feel the power and authority in that name. Oh, how wonderful it is to get to know Him and experience His glory!

God's word is all you need to keep your faith strong enough to get through this trial. You are right where he wants you to be so that he can pour himself into you. He gives you exactly what you need and who you need in your time of need. Believe that you are worthy and trust him. What a mighty God we serve! I am getting excited just thinking about him right now!

I wish I could say that those previous chapters you read were the only struggles and heartache I experienced, but whew child! There was more to come. I have more to testify about! After my son Keyon passed, my life started taking hit after hit! My first marriage was next on the hit list. I call it a hit list because it was one thing after another that was trying to destroy me mentally and physically.

Our finances took a blow and that put a strain on our relationship. We argued over small things almost every day and began to grow apart. My husband and I would separate and get back together. This went on for a few years. I wanted us to remain a family but just didn't know how to stop our conflict. I prayed to God to save my marriage, but God had another plan. Sometimes while I was in the middle of my prayer, I'd feel the presence of God telling me to get rid of the "dead weight." I didn't understand the message at first, but He kept showing me every time that my husband and I would separate, my finances would improve. God even spoke through my sister who told me that I was better off without my husband. I heard the message but was still holding on to something God was telling me to let go of.

One thing that made me hesitate about moving on without my husband was being stuck in my religious thinking; believing that God was totally against divorce. Thinking that way caused me to be miserable and stagnant in my marriage. I know for sure that God does not want us to live that way.

During this time, I was taking a prophetic class where we had to prophesy to one another. A minister from another church who I've never seen before stood up and pointed to me and said, "I see you praying in your prayer closet every night." What he said next blew my mind! In a firm voice, he said, "Get rid of that dead weight." If I didn't believe in the prophecy then, that would have made me a believer! I can smile about that now because it is more confirmation that God will use others to get his message to you. He is the same God who told me I was my husband's wife, and he is the same God who told me to get rid of him. Only God can do such things and make it right in your life and for His kingdom.

I learned the sovereignty of God through this. Because I had believed that once you get married you stay married, only God could set me free from that thinking. God had me reading Romans 7 and He showed me he is sovereign and that he can do what needs to be done to advance the kingdom of God.

Now, here I am divorced with two kids and unsure of what

is next for my life, but I was reminded that God knows the plans and purpose. At that time, I sought the Lord like never before. We often forget that God is the author and finisher of our faith. He is in control of our lives whether we trust him or not. I didn't know it at the time, but God was leading me into a new season of experiencing more of who he is and the power of his name.

I went through a season of loss. One year, my son died. Then the next year and a half, I got divorced. Right after that we lost the house and car. We had to move into a two-bedroom apartment. Sometimes our electricity or water would get cut off because we couldn't pay those bills. I'd still go to work every day with a smile on my face like everything was fine. Even around family and friends, I didn't let on to my problems. No one knew anything. I kept going to church, praising God, and going back home to no electricity.

I was still praying, sowing, fasting, and believing in God for a breakthrough. I'd charge my cell phone in the car or wherever we happened to be before heading home. We got used to a dark apartment and using flashlights at home. Instead of a refrigerator, we used a cooler to keep things cold, and the kids and I ate out for most of the meals. I kept tabs of all the places where kids ate at a discount—at one restaurant, kids ate free on Tuesdays; at another, it was Fridays. As a mother, I had to figure out a way for us to survive in this world even when things felt like they were against me.

I remember one time in prayer I cried out to God for help or some kind of relief. I was so frustrated that I yelled out, "Why did you give me these kids, and I can't take care of them?" I was tired of struggling. All I wanted was to take care of my kids, pay my bills, and have some peace of mind. I couldn't understand why I struggled so badly with my finances. I was not a big spender, and I only bought what we needed. I never got my hair done in a salon, and whenever the kids or I needed new clothing, it was second hand from a relative or the church. I discovered that God blesses others so that they can bless you.

My mother is that blessing in my life. I thank God for her. She has always been there for me—whatever I needed I just called and asked her, and she would help us. She paid our bills and bought whatever else the kids needed. I could count on her. I love that woman so dearly! She's not only my mother but also my best friend.

Every year during Christmas time, my church has a program with toys and gifts for the kids. And that year we won the toy raffle. That was a huge blessing because I had been praying for a pleasant holiday for my kids because I could not afford anything for them. God answered my prayers. God is so good and he knows your need before you even have the need. He provides it right on time. God will blow your mind just as he did for us that Christmas.

A year had gone by, and our lease was up. We couldn't renew it, so we had nowhere to go. My son Keymonie was already living with his father because he was causing trouble at school. And my daughter and I moved in with my momma. I questioned why it felt as if God had forsaken me. I was sort of joking about that, but I was thinking on that level. I was thirty-something years old and moving back in with my momma. I hate that I had to do that, but I had no other options. I was mad at myself for being in this situation. I'd stay out late to avoid going home or would even spend the night elsewhere sometimes. I love my momma and appreciate everything she's done for us, but moving back in with her as an adult was not easy. This was another hit.

I prayed and prayed for God to open another door for us to have our own place again. I searched for several months until I came across a place that accepted applicants with evictions on their credit. Glory be to God! I knew that this was for me, and it was back on the eastside where my daughter attended school. I was tired of living with my momma and tired of driving from the west side to the east side of town every weekday. I learned how to depend on God during this time to make a way for us. I was believing in God for a breakthrough.

Growing up, I watched my mother work three jobs to make ends meet. It was just her and me until she married so I know the adversity of growing up in a single-parent household. My mother worked her main job at the hospital, then she'd come home to change clothes, and then went to her second job where she cooked at a restaurant. On Saturdays, she cooked at another restaurant all day long. Back then, I witnessed her struggle to take care of me and the household. I also got to witness God deliver my mother from her hardships, and He granted her a greater life that she is living now. She owns her own home and has a catering business. She and her husband own two cars, and my mother is no longer struggling. God truly is blessing her. I pray that He continues to keep her and show her favor.

During that time of living with my mother again, I learned to rely even more on my Father God in heaven. He opened the door for us to have our own place once more. We moved into a three-bedroom apartment, and my son came from his father's house to live with my daughter and me. Keymonie was going to be a freshman in high school, and my daughter was starting first grade that year. Life was starting to look up again, but the struggle was still real. I was catching blows in all areas of my life. Not just financially. I had a hard time with parenting. Sometimes my kids were so rebellious, and they thought they knew everything. Both were getting into trouble at school and had teachers calling home. It felt like my life was out of control.

It's said that God will not put more on you than you can handle. He must have thought I was Wonder Woman because it was battle after battle for years of my life. I prayed for relief, but He kept me in the fire. It seemed as if the heat was turned up a little more with every trial. Another hit came in the form of another eviction. Once again, I had no idea where we were going to live. That night I prayed for God to provide somewhere for us to go. I put my trust in Him, and as difficult as it was, I didn't allow myself to worry. That morning, God made a way. He put it on my auntie's heart to open her doors to us until we could get our own place. God provided for us again!

Keymonie was having trouble at school more often. I was still going through financial hardship, and on top of that my family was persecuting me. Most of my family turned their backs on me all because of a lie that was told. Being persecuted is hard, but when it comes from the people you love, the hurt runs deeper. We spent time together almost every weekend eating, laughing, and enjoying one another's company. It took one snake to slither into our family and break up that closeness. I was mad, hurt, and disappointed in my family, and I dealt with the emotional pain of that for years.

God told me to let it go and forgive them, and that wasn't easy. First, I had to find out what the lie was to hold someone accountable. Then I confronted the family members, which didn't go well. Sometimes people can't be honest with you because they haven't been honest with themselves. Every time we had a family gathering there was tension in the air. Some family members wouldn't speak to me, some would stare at me, and others laughed at me. But God watches how you handle situations like that. As a lover of God, you have a responsibility to love others, even when they don't love you the same.

One day in my prayer time I was instructed to forgive all the people who hurt me in the past. I apologized to my family first, and then I told them that I forgave them too. God wants us to love our enemies and pray for those who persecute us. Not only that, but God also wants us to bless them. Even when you know the word and what you are *supposed* to do, it can still be challenging at times to turn the other cheek.

Of course, forgiveness is easier said than done. And it's also easier to stay mad at others, but that is not of God. You'll have to deal with it one way or another if you are to be the godly person He created us to be. If you ignore it, or feed into that negativity, it will become a heart issue. Not forgiving others can take root in your heart and cause sickness, and it can also block your blessings. Forgiveness is for you because forgiveness is of God. I had to forgive and let go so that I could have my peace back. And that's exactly what I did; I let it go and took back my peace. My relationship with those family members is better now, but it's still not like it was, which is fine because that was God's plan.

Despite all that, I kept serving and praising Him. God opened a new door for us to rent a three-bedroom house. The kids were doing better at school and at home, and my finances had gotten better. I learned to depend on God more. I learned to trust him in different areas of my life. Often, we trust God with some things or certain areas of our lives but not with all things. But if we think about it honestly, God's track record proves that he is trustworthy with *all* things.

Sit back and think about some of the trials you've been through in the past and how He brought you through them. Allow your faith and your trust to increase and be encouraged by the Lord each time he delivers you. Have the courage to keep on going and have faith in God to get you there. I know I did!

Another thing I learned was how to relinquish my hold on to things. When I say "relinquish," I mean to give up; retreat from; to release. Once we learn how to relinquish and trust God wholeheartedly there will be nothing we can't have or do for the kingdom of God. You must speak and walk in faith and then you'll see how it will work out for your good. It was hard for me to let things go, but I had to for my own healing. God kept telling me to get out from among others and separate myself. I didn't listen, so He did the separating.

I kept pressing on and living my life. Things were not always favorable, but it was not all bad either. Life was teaching me lessons and God were having His way. I was serving God and doing my best to live a life that's pleasing to Him. This takes me back to a prayer that I prayed when I first grew closer to God. I prayed and asked Him to use me. I told God I'll go where he wants me to go, do what he wants me to do, and say what he wants me to say. I was crazy in love and on fire for Him. There was nothing I wouldn't do for God.

I was in church every time the doors were open. I just love praising God and being in his presence. The love that I have for God caused me to want to give my all to Him. That is what you will do for someone you love. You are willing to do anything for them. I meant what I said then, and I still mean it now. When you love and worship God like that, He can trust you with anything. You will be used in all kinds of ways for the kingdom of God. God will use you in ways others can't even imagine. It will look crazy from the outside, but it will be ok with you. Let go of what you think others are thinking about you and trust God's assignment for you.

Remember what I said before about watching what you pray for? It's like when you study a subject in school. First, the teacher writes the lesson. Next, the students read that lesson. Then, the teacher gives more insight into the lesson, which is when the students gain information and understanding. Next comes the test that assesses your growth and understanding of what you were taught. The word of God is truth, and he is ready to see how true you are to Him and His word.

I continued to ask God to use me. And one day in 2018 I felt that I served that purpose. I was taking a shower praying for my husband, amongst other things. I asked God to tell me his name. Then God started speaking back. He told me his name. Some months later I was out celebrating a cousin's birthday having a great time with family and friends, and I met a man by that same name. Under God's will, that man became my second husband.

He was not the type of man that I would have chosen for myself, but I understood the assignment. After meeting him, I prayed and asked God if this was the man he was talking about for marriage. God didn't answer right away, but when he did, he said, "Yes." But that was all he said, or at least all that I understood. Either God did not finish the conversation, or it was me who left the conversation early. To this day I am not sure what happened, but I believe that if he had finished that conversation, I probably would have opted out of the assignment knowing the result. We divorced after one year.

From this marriage, I think God used me to bring my ex-husband closer to Him—or for him to see God in a different way because you never know what another person is praying for from God. God used me this time!

Let one of your goals be to be a vessel for the mighty hand of God.

The pandemic hit us all in 2020. People all around the world were feeling the ups and the downs together. Only God can allow something like that to happen and cause it to work for our good. There were famine, sickness, job losses, and death during that time, but God was faithful, and he brought us through it all.

I trusted God and declared His word over my family that COVID would not come near us nor to our dwelling place. I declared that COVID-19 was not for us, and we made it through it. I did not walk in fear of *what if*. I trusted God through it all for me and my family. God was gracious and merciful towards us during that time.

As challenging as the pandemic was, it did give me time to think and allowed space to analyze myself and where I was in life. I believe God gave all of us that time to reflect and evaluate ourselves. That season, for some, was like a reset where we were able to get things in order mentally and emotionally as well as draw closer to God. Blessings came out from the pandemic as well!

Keymonie graduated from high school that year. We thank God for blessing us and bringing us through! When the world returned to "normal," we were able to go back to work and church and socialize again. In this season, God elevated me in many areas of my life.

For about ten years I had been believing in God for my own home. And I acted on that faith buying new pieces for my future living room and other little things I wanted to have. I also started packing up things and selling some of my furniture believing that a new home would be mine despite not having any physical proof or reason to do so. I didn't have the money, but I had a word from God, and I believed him.

During the pandemic, I was able to repair my credit enough to get pre-approved for a home loan. I searched for a house on the west side of town for about six months, but God had other plans for me. One day I finally asked God where he wanted me to live. As soon as I relinquished my plan and asked God His plan, I found the house he had for me. It was right across the street from the house I lived in when I first moved out east in 2007.

My God is a restorer, and he knows how to bring blessings back if you weren't ready for them the first time around. I thank God that He is in control. God knows what he is doing. He will work it all out. He did it for me and he will do it for you. On the closing day of the house, I needed more money. And God worked it out at the closing table. He touched the seller's heart to give the extra funds that I needed to purchase the home!

Remember that what is for you, it is for you.

He did it for me, and he will do it for you! You must trust God's timing even when it looks as if it is not going to happen; even when you are at the eleventh hour. God is an on-time God! He shows up right when you need him to show up and he never fails. If God said it or showed it to you, believe you will have it!

It's important to keep in mind that our steps are ordered by the Lord. God knows exactly where you are and how to get you to where you need to be. All we need to do is listen, trust, and obey. God's word is a lamp unto our feet and a light unto our pathway. God says in His word that He knows the way we should go. If we are willing and obedient we will eat the goods of the land. I don't know about anybody else but the way my life had been going I was ready for all the blessings that God had for me.

I finally saw some joy, and I was feeling positive about my life. Sometimes life's challenges can be so hard that you can't see your way out or see the light at the end of the tunnel. It will have you wondering when the shift will happen or feeling as if it will never happen. But I am a witness. I am seeing and living the goodness of God in my life.

Trust God's timing for your life.

My kids were happy that we finally moved into our own place and their faith in God increased. They began to lose hope in the moving process because it was taking so long, but I didn't. I knew it was going to happen! They got the chance to see how God came through on his promise and now we're living it! God said that after you have suffered a little while, He will establish you, strengthen you, and settle you, and he did just that for my family.

Our two-story, three-bedroom, two-car garage home was a dream come true. All our needs were met, and I had more income than ever. God was showing up and showing out in my life! I was even able to bless other people financially; some I knew personally and others I didn't know at all. We were living in the overflow, so I let it run over to others. I couldn't complain about anything because all was well. To God be the glory!

This kind of season increases faith in God more when you see your prayers being answered and things start to come together for you. When you see the mighty hand of God in your life fixing and causing things to work together for your good, it gives you more confidence to speak more things into existence. A season like this also builds your understanding of how to tap into the power that God gave you and have dominion over things in your life.

When you study God's word and believe it in your heart, there may come a time that the word in your heart will be tested so the truth of you can be revealed. These last couple of tests almost destroyed me, but God said not my child!

When tests and trials come into your life, pray and ask God to let His will be done. I say this so that if you don't see your prayer be answered in the way or the time that you think it should be, know that God's will never fails. After you put your petition before God say, "Nevertheless, God let your will be done in Jesus Name!"

Look at what Jesus did at Gethsemane; he prayed to God for the cup to pass over him. Jesus recognized God as sovereign so he knew God's will trumped his own. So, Jesus submitted and accepted God's will by saying, "Nevertheless let your will be done." That word "nevertheless" surrenders or submits your will to God's will.

I have been blessed with a lot of knowledge over the course of my journey, but that is one of the most important things I learned about prayer. I learned to accept the word and the will of God for my life. I took some difficult hits during 2022 and 2023, but God was with me through them all. His plan and his purpose are perfect. It may not be easy, but God puts you in a position to win in the end.

Again, I say TRUST THE PROCESS!

The year 2022 started off alright. I had the typical issues as a single parent and a woman of God. It's not easy wearing multiple hats and being there for everyone, but God gives us the strength to accomplish what needs to be done. We can run and hide in him, knowing we will be safe there. So, when the storm comes, God will hide you under his wings. I know this because I am still living it.

Later that year I started dating again. I was believing in God for a suitable helper. I met a guy younger than me and at first,

I was hesitant about being involved with him. But he treated me better than any man in my past ever had. He was mature and seemed responsible, and he knew how to treat a woman. I never had a man honor me and put me first before. He catered to me and showed me things in a relationship that I had always dreamed of. He let me see clearly the type of man I wanted in my life. I believe God used him and that relationship to show me how I should be treated, and it gave me hope to wait on my Boaz. He was a good man; he just wasn't the husband God had for me.

After he and I broke up, I had a conversation with one of my male cousins and he reminded me that I talk to God about sending me the right person for a relationship but that I hadn't prayed to *be* the right person for a relationship. That really took me by surprise, but I needed to hear it. So, guess what I did that night? I sat down and prayed. Then I started searching within and let God reveal *me to myself*. I knew that I had to change and grow and prepare for the man God was sending to me.

I spent the remainder of that year working on me and examining the enemy that was within. I was intentional about being a better cook. I was taking care of my household in a more elevated way; keeping things clean and organized and making sure bills were paid on time. I wanted to prepare to be a virtuous wife for my husband. I wanted him, whoever he was, to come into my life and add to my peace, and I add to his. I worked on everything within myself that I could think of.

If you really want to change, God will help you. He will reveal things about yourself that you have the power to change. He will guide you to become the best version of yourself.

Keymonie had gotten into trouble being in the streets and with law enforcement. This brought a lot of stress into my life. I worried about paying for lawyers to represent him and putting money in his books while he was incarcerated all while taking care of my daughter and our home. I was scared for my son because of the life he was living, but I had to be strong for him and my daughter. I stayed on my knees in prayer, believing God for a victorious turn around in Keymonie's life.

His lifestyle was catching up with him and brought trouble to our doorstep. One morning at the end of that summer, my house was shot up from top to bottom. Keymonie had just got home and had gone upstairs to his room. That's when the gunshots started. Thankfully, an hour before that, my cousins and I had just left the house. If we had been home at that time, we all would have been downstairs in the living room, right in the crossfire. Later, the police said that three different shooters shot from the back of the house through to the front. There were over forty-five rounds of bullets scattered throughout our home. Glory be to God; my children were unharmed! It was only God's protection around this house that no one was struck.

After hearing about the shooting that morning, I rushed home and all I could do was praise God. Bullet holes were found on almost every wall and window in the house. But I noticed not one bullet came near my kids' beds. There were bullet holes in the legs of my kitchen table and through the baseboards of the walls, on both levels of the house. No one would have been safe inside of that house even if they were on the floor. But He knew how to protect me. At first, I was mad at myself for not being home and questioned why God didn't have me there to protect my children.

That Sunday, I was taking a nap after getting home from church. I woke up to gunfire ringing in my ear. It sounded so real that it woke me from my sleep, and I ran to my bedroom door to check on my kids. As soon as I touched the doorknob, the Lord spoke and said that is why you weren't home. When I opened my bedroom door, I noticed all the bullet holes right outside my room. God knew I would have rushed to my kids when I heard those shots. I would have been shot up if God had not taken me out of that house. God is omniscient. He is all knowing!

He protects us and keeps us from things seen and unseen.

I also learned that we as parents can't hold too tightly trying to protect our kids. We do our best to teach them our morals and values, and then we must put them in God's hands and pray for His protection over them. The night of that shooting, I had some of the best sleep in years over at a friend's house. It was as if God was showing me that he'd give me rest during a storm. That next morning, my sister came banging on the door of my friend's house to let me know what transpired at my house. I remember when she told me, my heart stopped for a second before asking about the kids. She assured me that they were fine. People were calling my cell phone for hours, and I was sleeping so deeply that I did not hear it ring one time.

One the way home that morning my mind was racing back and forth. One moment I was mad at my son for allowing this to happen, thinking about all those times he had his friends over at my house. The next moment I was grateful that no one was hurt. Then I was mad again at the people who shot up my house. Once I reached home, and saw my kids and some of the damage, I let all that anger go and was just grateful. I stood in my living room, and all I could do was lift my hands in praise, thanking God for His protection.

Keymonie seemed to understand the gravity of the situation and apologized to me. I forgave him and held him tight. He is not perfect, and he lived the street life, but I love him and will do anything for him. He saw how his lifestyle made its way to our front door with his little sister inside. I believe that really shook him up. I held him tighter and prayed that he never found out who shot up our house.

Many family members told me to put my son out to keep my daughter and me safe. They told me that his actions would get us hurt. A lot of people will have things to say when it's not them or their child. I heard about how they could have, should have, or would have done this or that if they were in my shoes. After a while I had heard enough and had to remind them that God gave me my son and that I was doing all I could to take care of him.

This was not Keymonie's first-time causing trouble, so my family looked down upon us because of what he was doing in the world. One thing they didn't understand was that I would never turn my back on my kids no matter what. My passion for my children runs deeply and is a part of who I am, who

God made me to be. Many people had a lot to say about my son, but I had to draw the line especially since none of them were there to help me guide him or show him how to be an honorable man. Since his father wasn't around, Keymonie (like most kids) had to figure out how to find that masculine guidance and unfortunately it came from the streets. He was doing his best trying to figure it out.

The night of the shooting, my mom stayed over at the house with us. She was the comfort that I needed. And that was the last time I slept somewhere else other than my home. God said he will protect and restore us, and he did just what he said. Everything that was damaged during the shootout was things that I wanted to change anyway. Keep in mind that what the devil meant for evil, God turned it around for my good. He said he will repair the holes, replace the broken windows, and make all things new. I was in prayer one morning shortly after that and God led me to a scripture: Amos 9:11-12. God continued to blow my mind!

There is a scripture in the Bible for everything we experience in life. The answer to your questions or problems is in the word of God. He knows our beginning and our end and everything in between. God restored our house, and it was like new.

Even during that time of restoring my house, God had me

on another mission. He inspired me to gather women to go to a conference called Women Thou Art Loosed in Atlanta, Georgia. At first this assignment sounded perfect, and I believed that I could accomplish it. Things were unfolding smoothly. I sent out the invitations to several women and booked our tickets based on the number of confirmations. I had it all planned out, and we got a group discount for our tickets through my program, God's Wonderful Woman. The rooms were reserved and the transportation was arranged.

Two weeks out of the event is when things started to take a turn. A few women could no longer go, but the real drama came the day before it was time for us to leave for the conference. I went to the rental car place to pick up the van, and the credit card was declined. I used another card and that one didn't work either. My first thought was that the credit card machine was broken. Then I figured with such a powerful group of women, the devil was trying to deter us from attending. After leaving the rental place with no van and getting home, another woman called to say that she could no longer attend. We went from seventeen women to only four of us going to Georgia. I had a passing thought that almost made me panic, but then God intervened. He put it in my spirit to call and ask my mother if I could drive her SUV to Atlanta. I was nervous because I know how my mother is with her car, but glory be to God she said yes.

Thank you, Lord, for making a way!

We got to Atlanta, and my credit card still didn't work to check in at the hotel. But God had a ram in the bush. The ladies were able to pay for their rooms that day. I was thankful but still did not understand what was going on because I know I had the money in my bank account. My heart was heavy because I worried about what the ladies thought of me. When we got to the conference, I decided to let go of those thoughts. I couldn't fix it, so I had to stop worrying and instead praise God for getting us there safely. The next morning, I realized that my account was on hold because of the insurance check for my house. They released my account, and I was able to give the ladies back their money. I had been waiting on this money for months to get my house repaired. I wanted it done before I went out of town, but Glory be to God that he had everything worked out.

His will is perfect for my life. God knows when and how to bless His people.

The conference was so impactful; I got delivered from the enemy, and my strength was renewed. God showed up at that event, and all was well. God's Wonderful Woman sponsored the women to attend the conference that year. We were also able to be a blessing to seven single mothers and their children that Christmas. What a blessing it is to be a blessing! I asked family and friends to donate so we could give support to single mothers in the community. I know firsthand how hard it is to care for your kids with little day-to-day help and not have anything for them at Christmas.

I love being able to take away the stress, pain, and hurt from people through the power of giving. Whether I am giving something physically or sharing the good news of Jesus, I believe that to be the sole purpose of becoming the woman God wants me to be. Through my nonprofit, I aim to help lighten the load for single mothers. I think back to when I was in that position and it meant so much when someone came to my aid. All I needed was just a little assistance with daycare, food, utilities, or housing. Just helping with one of those expenses made a world of difference.

The system that is meant to assist single mothers would often turn us down because we didn't qualify on every level—maybe we earn a dollar over the poverty level, or our children are too close in age, or in my case, I had a full-time job and a degree. As a single mother, we only see that our needs exceed our wages, and we need a little help with monthly expenses. That kind of assistance fosters healthier households in our communities. Thankfully now, through Christ, God's Wonderful Woman can be a source of strength and support that helps ease the burdens of other working single mothers.

5

THE SHIFT

Saying, Father, if thou be willing, remove this cup from me: nevertheless, not my will but thine, be done.
Luke 22:42

At the beginning of 2023, I declared to God that I would be getting married that October. I had been speaking and standing on God's word (Genesis 2:18) where he said he will go make you a suitable helper. God gave me a revelation about my suitable helper in the form of an analogy; He said when you go to the tailor for a custom suit, no one can fit that suit but you. It is fit for your exact measurements, perfect for you in every area. No one could even try it on, let alone wear it. It is made and designed for only you. That's your suitable helper.

When I made that declaration, I was single—no man, no prospects, nothing. However, I had been working on myself preparing for that man. I was positioning myself emotionally and spiritually to be the right woman for that right man that God had for me. I prayed to be a suitable helper for him too.

I had faith that he was on his way. The confidence to speak certain things over your own life is a gift from God that allows Him to show his mighty hand. I spoke His word, and I believed it in my heart so with that belief came action. Almost half the year had gone by and still I had no prospects. Since I wanted to be married by October I talked to God as if I was talking to a close friend: "Come on now, the end of the year is getting close. Can we at least meet each other soon?"

June had come and my sisters were getting ready for their annual girls trip. I considered going, but one night while I was still on the fence about it, the Holy Spirit put it on my heart to join a dating app. I had never used a dating app before, but I went where I was led and joined one. It was strange and new, and I was nervous just thinking about meeting someone this way. The day that I signed up for the app I was instantly matched with Mr. Milan Harris. I messaged him that night and went to bed for the night. I woke up to a message from him and from that initial contact, I knew he was my suitable helper. That Friday night we agreed to get off the app because the feeling that we both found our person was mutual. We talked and laughed on the phone all night. He wanted to meet up that weekend, so I invited him to my church's fish fry on Saturday. I let him know that if he really wanted to see me, he would have to come to church and buy me a fish dinner.

What better place to meet than at church where it was safe and my church family could also size him up for me. I told my Bishop what transpired that week and that I wanted his opinion of this man. He laughed and agreed. Milan arrived, and I was a bit nervous, so I immediately introduced him to my Bishop. They chatted and we all got to know him. The conversation was so organic and just flowed that I forgot I was supposed to be helping to plate the fish dinners. After that weekend, we started dating and hanging out often. We prayed together and separately and asked God about each other. God spoke to each of us about the other. Milan asked me to marry him a month later in July, and I said yes!

The time had come to plan our wedding. My dress and the bridesmaids' dresses had been chosen at the beginning of the year when I made the declaration to be married in October. When I told my sisters that I was getting married in a few months, naturally they were shocked. They had their opinions, but they were willing to be a part of the wedding and to spend the next few months getting to know Milan to see what he was all about. He met my mom's and dad's sides of the family, and he fit in perfectly, just like a helpmate does. Insert chapter five text here. Insert chapter five text here. Insert chapter five text here. Insert chapter five text here.

God sent Milan into my life at the right time in the right

way. My kids loved him too! Even Keymonie surprised me because he's the type to stay out of my business unless there's a problem. But he came to me one day and said, "Momma, he's cool. I like him for you." Kimmyah is different. She is very hard to please and wants her momma all to herself. It shocked me when she talked to him the first time they met. I talked to the kids about getting married, and they both were fine with it. My kids seemed to enjoy getting to know Milan and they formed their own bonds with him. The kids were excited about being a part of the wedding: Keymonie as a groomsman and Kimmyah as a bridesmaid. They were going to walk down the aisle together and carry Keyon's picture, but God had another plan.

On August 25, 2023, my oldest son Keymonie William Allen was killed. He was shot in broad daylight. It was a hot summer day at about two in the afternoon. I will never forget that day.

I was working from home sitting at my desk when my nephew called. He shouted through the phone, "Keymonie has been shot, please go help him!" My heart dropped. I wasn't sure that I heard what I thought I heard, but deep down, I knew. After we hung up the phone, I called my son to see if he would answer. I kept calling his phone and it kept ringing. My heart was racing, and I called my nephew back and that's when he told me that Keymonie was gone. At that point I was freaking out because Keymonie had been shot before, and he survived. I was hoping and praying that this was another one of those times.

I hopped in my car driving as fast as I could to the apartments that my nephew said Keymonie was in. In between crying I prayed aloud to God asking him to save my baby and reminding Him that I already buried one son. "God, if you take him, then I have no more sons." I reminded God of my service to him and that I had been praying for Him to deliver my boy daily. I wanted God to do what I knew he could do. From this experience I learned that I have no choice but to accept His will for my life. text here. Insert chapter five text here.

My phone was ringing off the hook with friends and family trying to find out if it was true. Once I arrived at the apartment complex, I saw yellow tape, one police car, and a Chaplin. I jumped out of the car and ran over to them asking what happened to my son and why the ambulance was not there yet! They didn't answer my questions but tried to calm me down. Nothing could calm me down. I was so distraught that I ran through those apartments screaming and hollering. I was ready to go to war with everyone. Anyone I saw, I stopped and asked them if they saw who shot my son.

Some time had passed by before a woman found me and said that she would show me where Keymonie laid so that I could identify him. As soon as I turned the corner, I could see his shoes, and I knew it was my son. All I could do was scream his name. I got as close as I could to him by getting low to the ground shouting, "Keymonie, get up! It's your momma! Get up, Keymonie!" I couldn't believe this was happening again to our family! I was at a loss for words and angry at the same time.

Family and friends began showing up. Both my parents' sides of the family were there along with my son's father and his friends. My mind was all over the place. I was angry and I wanted justice. I wanted that person who killed my son to die! I had murder on my mind but thank God He is a mind regulator. God kept me from ruining my life and others around me.

While all this was happening, my daughter was still at school and didn't know about her brother yet. I wanted to be the one to tell her, but I couldn't leave my son lying on that ground. My aunt picked up Kimmyah from the bus stop by our house when she got home from school. Emotions were high all around me. People were crying and even began arguing with one another. I became numb, muted, and anguished. My beloved was gone.

The police moved the yellow tape due to the growing crowd and as soon as they did, I sprinted to the spot where my baby's body was lying. I wanted to hold my child one more time, but when I got next to him, I noticed a swarm of flies going in and out his mouth. That startled me and I jumped back. The police were close behind and pulled me away from him. I didn't care about the evidence or anything, I just wanted my son.

The police urged everyone in the vicinity to leave while they processed the crime scene. But I couldn't leave my baby there. Keymonie's friends were mad and some were crying. I had never seen so much hurt in these young men's faces. It hurt me even more to see them crying for their friend. Many of them paced back and forth with their shirts off, shouting with weapons holstered to their hips. These kids were so mad they didn't care about the police being there, they wanted revenge. We were there so long that one of my cousins left and came back with food for everyone. Nobody left until they took Keymonie away.

I had Facetimed with my son about an hour before he was shot so the shock and disbelief was overwhelming. He was at a different place when I talked to him, and everything seemed fine. I called him early that morning because his mentor knocked at the door because they were supposed to meet up.

When I called to let him know I didn't think he was going to answer, but he did. We started laughing and joking about him being up so early. He asked me to bring him some food, but I was already on the clock for work so I couldn't. Then Keymonie called me asking if I could do his friend's hair, but I was still working. Oh, how I wish I had said yes. Sometimes I think if I had said yes, he would have been home at that time, and he would still be alive.

One of the detectives talked to me for a few minutes, gave me his card, and I left the scene. I drove myself home in shock that I was about to bury another child. *Again Lord! Again Lord?! Do you remember what I went through last time God?* I was BIG MAD and heartbroken! I don't know how I drove home with my eyes filled with tears. I felt another hole in my heart. My phone rang nonstop and my anxiety was through the roof. It felt as if I couldn't breathe. The closer I got home, the more I began to gasp for air, and I couldn't catch my breath. My breathing was faster and more labored. I wanted to scream. I wanted my baby back!! I had already buried my baby son in 2012 and now I was doing it again in 2023. I couldn't understand why I was going through this again! God's ways are not our ways, and his thoughts are not our thoughts. He knows the purpose and plans he has for us, and they are not to harm but to give us an expected end. This was his plan, and

I must live it out.

There was so much controversy surrounding Keymonie's death and how it happened. The rumor around town was that someone in his family set him up, and some said that his friends set him up. It made me remember a time when Keymonie told me that if anything ever happened to him it would be in the hands of somebody he knew. We still don't know the truth behind what really happened to him. What I do know is that my son is gone, and there has yet to be any justice for his murder. I am believing God for justice.

Planning another funeral for one of my kids was so hard for me I couldn't even think straight. All I wanted was my son back with me. I really didn't have the energy to plan the funeral, but I masked it and kept going. I was just doing things out of routine because I had to do them. I was angry every day that I woke up to this nightmare. And I wanted to kill the person who did this. I felt as if my life was over. I wanted to die every day. Anger was controlling me. Hurt was devouring me! Pain was eating me alive! I couldn't find any peace.

My anger toward God was so intense that I didn't even want to pray. I wasn't even talking to Him anymore, all I did was cry. I also drank alcohol and smoked weed like it was going out of style. In the mornings when I woke up, I'd almost feel normal then the realization would hit me; my son was gone.

I'd feel the pain of losing him all over again. I was mad at the world, God, and everyone that had something to do with it. My pain was so deep it scared me sometimes because I didn't care about anything but my son. My fiancé tried to console me, but he couldn't take away the pain. I didn't care what anybody said. I didn't want to hear nothing about God. Anger consumed me completely.

I prayed to God to help deliver Keymonie from the streets, but I didn't know God was going to do it this way. Sounds familiar? Just like with my baby son, God has his own way of doing things, and as hard as it is all we can do is trust him. It took some time to get there, but I had to ask God to forgive me for that anger towards Him, and He did. Thank you, God, for restoring our relationship!

The colors for the funeral were black and red. My son's casket was black with chrome handles. I dressed him in a black suit, red shirt, and black bow tie. He was so handsome. I stood right by my son's casket for the entire ceremony, even as people walked by to view his body. Because of all the talk and rumors going on, I was not about to let anybody mess up his funeral or even touch him. Some people tried to cause confusion during the service, and they tried to stop it. I didn't allow any of that. My son was getting a proper funeral and burial service. My Bishop took control over the atmosphere, and we were able to finish what was started.

We got through that day even though it was rough; God kept us! After that, I needed to get away and clear my mind. All I did was cry every day. I couldn't even help my daughter with her grief because of mine. I thought maybe if we got away from home for a few days, we would feel better. A road trip always helped to clear my mind, so I wanted to do the same for my mom and daughter.

In October we took a family vacation that was much needed for all of us. My family, Milan, and I drove to Atlanta for my aunt's birthday and to meet Milan's family. On the drive there, the car my mom was riding in was side swiped by a semitruck, but God protected them. All was well! My mom was sore, but she was ok. That same truck almost rear-ended the car we were in. I braced myself and called out, "JESUS!" I just knew he was going to slam into us, but God stepped in and intervened.

It was important to meet Milan's family before we got married, and it seemed as if the enemy was trying to keep us from getting to Atlanta. When it finally happened, it was amazing. Everyone connected like we had known one another for years. Only God can create that feeling. We had a great three days in Atlanta, and Milan's mother gave her blessing for us to wed. I couldn't ask for a better union. We all returned home safely ready to finish planning the wedding.

I almost called it off because I was not feeling the excitement of getting married. My son's murder almost took the life out of me, but God had his own plans. Even though I did not want to go on with life and didn't have the joy or the energy to get married, God's plan still had to go forth. At the start of the year, I spoke the word into existence that I was getting married by the end of the year and believed it. It was on God to bring it to pass.

Even when we do not know what will happen during the waiting period for His word to come to pass, know that God's word will forever stand and what he proclaims shall be seen by all.

It was crunch time and my sisters and I were preparing for this wedding. Our date was set for December 16, and we only had a month to get things ready. My sisters are the best! They came together and got everything done for me. I had only chosen the wedding colors and had the bridesmaids' dresses picked out. The dress that I ordered for myself was too small and there was no time to send it back to get another size. My frustration began to rise because I really didn't have the money to buy a new one, and I still had to get my daughter's dress, but God came through again. Kimmyah found her dress and I got a beautiful one that was tailormade for me. I give all glory to God because when it is His will *everything* has to obey.

Milan and I found the venue and catering that met our budget. My sisters found a wonderful photographer and the event went off without a hitch. We had a lovely wedding! Everything was perfect from beginning to end. Even the weather was perfect despite it being December. God's hand was evident the entire time on our special day. God said he will raise up people with power and influence to help and bless you and He did just that! Altogether, we probably spent less than $5,000 on everything. My sisters took care of the bridal shower and the bridesmaids' party favors. I couldn't have done any of it without them. I just love them so much! My wedding was fabulous, and I was so happy that day.

At first, I didn't want to celebrate with a wedding ceremony, for obvious reasons, but I am so glad we did. I could feel both of my sons there in spirit. My daughter walked down the aisle holding a framed picture of my boys. It was sad and beautiful all at the same time. After the wedding we were blessed to get two vacation packages for the price of one and took our honeymoon a few months later in January. God will exceed your expectations if you let Him. I was off work for a few days after the wedding, and my husband and I enjoyed each other's company, doing what newlyweds do.

That Tuesday when I went back to work, I was fired. I had a feeling that it was coming because the boss told me more than once that I was messing up my work. But when the union investigated it, they found out that it was really her wrongdoing. I laughed with God because of his perfect timing. I was so glad that He waited until I got a husband.

When I started that job, I told myself that it would be my last before going into ministry full time. And that was God's plan as well. As I've said before, God will have you speaking things over your life that He also desires for you. And once you truly believe it and align with his will, God will perform just what you said.

I knew that more was meant for me. By the time our honeymoon came in January, we were so excited for this much-needed vacation. When we booked our honeymoon, there was a buy one, get one free deal that afforded us three vacation spots: Las Vegas, Disney World for four people, and a cruise. God showed us so much favor! We went to Las Vegas for our honeymoon and God joined us. We met some wonderful people who encouraged us while we were there. People shared with us their testimonies about starting businesses. These people were speaking life into us and motivated us to move forward in business and in life.

6

THE TRANSFORMATION

O wretched man that I am! Who shall deliver me from the body of this death?
Romans 7:25

Looking back over my life, God taught me that only He can deliver me from sin. Remember, you must be willing and ready to be delivered. It doesn't matter who you are or what you have done. God will save you and deliver you from you. We must be transformed from the things of this world into a new life in Christ.

"Change is inevitable," is what God spoke to me one day during my prayer time. When he spoke those words, fear came over me and I knew right then that it was about to go down. I felt the excitement of what was coming. Those words that God spoke to me started 'The You in You' challenge. I knew that this new chapter in my life was not going to be easy, but I knew that I could do all things through Christ because He is the one who strengthens me. If I want the new life in Christ that I had been praying for, I knew I had to let go of the old life. It was time to become the woman God called me to be and to do what He has called me to do.

The more time I spent with God, the more I trusted His calling. That call was greater than me. I've learned that the path of getting there was necessary. Every hurt, pain, struggle, death, and disappointment was what built me and led me to this moment in my life. Those experiences were unpleasant, but they served a purpose. I believe I went through those situations to be able to be a witness for the goodness of our Lord and Savior and to be proof to the world that he is faithful in all things.

When you find yourself going through struggle and strife, remember that God knows the plans and purpose he has set for your life. He has called you and set you apart for his great work.

Change comes into our lives for this exact reason: to set you apart and grow you. We must be aligned with God's plans and purpose and not get upset when things don't seem to go the way we planned. We must accept the changes that come into our lives, from friends to relationships. God will change your friend circle, and he will not allow you to fit in with certain crowds anymore. This is God's elevation and it may hurt at first. It's not until later that we can understand and give God glory for the change. To be the person God called me to be, I had to let go of the life that I once knew.

It's time to serve God with all your heart, mind, and soul.

There are people who have been assigned to your life; these people need what God has put in you. Your testimony will help others be delivered from their test. Change is inevitable! God showed me that he is a keeper even when I didn't want to be kept; even when I didn't think I deserved to be. During my adolescent years I wanted to do what I wanted to do. I wanted to live a life that I thought was best for me. So, when I was out there growing up in the streets, gang banging, selling drugs, and partying, God was the furthest thing from my mind. I thought I was having fun, but thankfully God was thinking about me.

God kept his angels encamped around me wherever I went. He kept me through shoot outs, fights, car accidents, abuse, police chases, and just being at the wrong place at the wrong time. God kept me in my coming and going in and out of trap houses, making drug transactions, and dealing with other drug dealers. Even as I became an adult, I was still doing things that were not pleasing to God, but He kept me, and his mercy is renewed every day. When I began to realize that God was with me, every time I went out to do whatever it was, I was doing, I knew to call on the name of Jesus and take him with me. I would say, "Jesus be with me," or "Jesus keep me," and He did just that. God kept and saved me through it all. He is Jehovah Hoshiah, the Lord who saves.

God ordered my steps. He led me right back to him every time. Every struggle and trial I had I called on his name to help me through it. He walks with me, and he talks with me. It was God guiding me to go here or not there. He led me away from strange places filled with danger. Even when I got off course, he led me right back to where I needed to be. He never let me go. God is the great shepherd! God will leave the ninety-nine and go after that one, which is you. We call him Jehovah Rohi, the Lord, my Shepherd.

God showed me that He is a healer. He showed me that he can heal any sickness and disease. When I had my baby son Keyon, God showed me in His word how he healed people on Earth. I grabbed those words and ran with it. I applied it to my baby who was stricken with an incurable disease. I knew God could heal him and nobody could tell me any different. I saw it in His word! I believed God and I knew He could do it. My faith was so strong that I had no doubts that God would perform a miracle for us. When the doctors said two years, God said seven.

When Keyon died, I lost my faith and trust in God. I was mad and disappointed for some time. I let that feeling sit in me too long that it affected my faith in God for the next thirteen years.

I struggled with believing in God. I believed God for everyone else, but I doubted him when it came to my life. That plagued my prayer life, and I went through some hard dark days because of it. God says in His word that it is impossible to please him without faith. During that time, the enemy planted a seed of doubt in me, and it almost destroyed me.

It seemed as if my blessings were hard to come by because of my lack of faith in God. Anytime I prayed about something, doubt would grow in my mind. A double-minded person should not expect to receive anything from the Lord. That battle for my faith led to a battle in my walk with God. But God is the author and finisher. He restored my faith in him again, and now my relationship with God is rooted in faith.

God will send healing for your soul.

Keep in mind, there are two kinds of healings from God. One is a healing that we can see and feel—the evidence in one's body or mind that they are no longer the same. People are made whole again. The other healing is when God calls you home to be with Him, and you are delivered from it all. Because in God there is no sickness, no pain, no hurt, no disease or anything that can cause you harm. In God, there is a resting place free from all things on Earth.

No matter how God heals you or a loved one, God is still the one who sends the healing. God is sovereign and we all belong to Him. He knows what we need and what is best for us. Even if God calls your loved ones home to Glory, we still must trust in Him. Receive and accept the healing God gives for your life (or loved ones) and know that he is "Jehovah Raphe," the Lord who heals.

God showed me that he is a protector. He protects us from the scheme and plots of the enemy when they desire our downfall. God protects us from seen and unseen dangers. He helps us to navigate through life with His word and his righteous hand. Everything that seems attractive and looks desirable is not always good for us. Sometimes you think you have it all figured out and you make plans, but God knows the end at the beginning. He foresees trouble and destruction. He sends his righteous hand to protect you from things you can't see. He is "Jehovah Magen," the shield.

I used to get mad when things didn't work out the way that I wanted. Like if I had a plan to get out of debt or to pay a bill by making a deal to get quick money, not knowing that the plan would lead me into more debt. Thank God that he sees all and knows all and that he protects us from our own ways of thinking and doing things. It's another reason why we should lean not on our own understanding but in all our ways acknowledge him so that he can direct our path. I learned to stay up under his mighty hand.

That time of struggle caused me to hate myself and to look at myself differently. I recognized that I was relying on myself, my job, and other people to provide for me, not God. Living that way created frustration and made me think it was never going to end. I learned to depend on God for everything. I had to be intentional about changing my mindset and looking at the hills for whence my help cometh. God had to break me down to nothing to teach me how to totally depend on Him.

Then God brought me to a time in my life where I had more than enough to be a blessing to others. In this new chapter, God called me away from my job and told me to go into ministry. Looking back, this was another opportunity to put my trust in Him. It was another struggle because I considered myself to be very independent. I like to be in control and hate having to owe people anything. So, when God delivered me from lack the last time, I vowed that I would never go back there again. But being in this position, in a place of not knowing and relying on my husband's income, really bothered me. I had to realize that I was not depending on my husband to provide for us; I was depending on the Lord. I shifted the way I was thinking.

God provided for every bill from mortgage to car payments and everything in between. Even when the payments were late, nothing was ever disconnected or sent to collections. God can sustain you and keep you from falling when you put your trust in Him. This transition from full-time work to my new role in ministry taught me to trust God like never before. If I didn't already know, this solidified that He is my provider! I can ask for a thing in Jesus's name, and I know that it is done. It all comes through Him. He is "Jehovah Jireh," which means the Lord will provide.

God showed me that he is a deliverer. I've witnessed God deliver me from so many storms and I've seen his righteous hand bring me out of darkness and into his marvelous light. God also delivered me from my own selfish ways and desires. I've seen God snatch me right out of the path of the enemy. When my oldest son died, I was in a very sorrowful place. I had no desire to live. I was furious and wanted to kill everybody, but God showed up and snatched me out of that gloomy place and showed me why I had to survive. God will deliver you out of the hard places.

You are not too far gone that God cannot bring you back.

God delivered me from the daily habits of smoking and drinking. I'd wake up to it and use it as a nightcap before bed. It kept me in a stupor. It kept me from moving forward in my walk with God. Those vices were distractions that the enemy used to take away my focus from God and what He has called me to do. I truly believed that I could not live without those things because they masked the pain, hurt, disappointments, pressure, and the afflictions I was facing. Marijuana and alcohol also drain the energy from you, making you constantly tired and unfocused. It will cause you to ignore your responsibilities and put off things that need to get done. The enemy's devices are all around and we think we are just enjoying life, but those temptations are keeping us from enjoying the life that God has blessed us with. I'm grateful that God delivered me from that way of living. I am so grateful because now I can see life through His eyes, and that helps me to live a life that is pleasing to Him.

God will deliver you in his timing because he knows when you are ready to walk the walk. There were so many times I tried to quit my vices and lay that life down. I would have a dream of me smoking or someone giving me a sack. After several times of living in that cycle, I learned that there was a set time for my deliverance. God will use you even while you are using.

I remember a time when I was out having fun at the club and God sent over someone for me to minister to. God is a master designer and will use you in your low situation to speak His words over others. I often think back to that time and know that if I wasn't smoking or drinking, I would not have been in that club to be able to minister to that person. At those same times something would happen that caused me to run back to my vices. I'd get some bad news or just the everyday stresses of life would happen, and I could never understand why it was so hard to leave it alone.

I realized that my vices weren't just mine, they were a part of a generational curse in my family. Curses follow families from generation to generation. God had to deliver me from things in my bloodline that kept me in bondage. Partying, drinking, and smoking were things that I grew up seeing all around me. I was born into sin and shaped into iniquity. Every weekend we would gather at a family member's house to eat, drink, and party. I believe that is why it was so hard for me to break these habits because it was around day in and day out. Once I grew up, I kept those same habits. But God has caused me to be a generational-curse breaker. I used to be the "the life of the party". I was the first one on the dance floor, but now I'm the first to break the generational curse for my family. He has chosen me for the greater good of my family, and I have answered the call!

God will deliver you from yourself.

When things get tough and rough for you, God will step in and deliver you. He knows how much you can take and what you can do, whether you think so or not. God is there to help and navigate you through it all. He is an on-time God! When you can't figure it out, turn to God because he already worked it out for you. God is never taken by surprise when trials surface in your life, whether they be death, loss of money, career troubles, marriage issues, health problems, or whatever it is. God declares the end at the beginning. You can trust Him with anything and everything in your life. You will see that it was only because of God that you are still here today.

God knows how to move you from depression or oppression to joy and peace. He knows how to get you to see it His way. God is also patient and concerned about how you are feeling. He lets you vent and be mad about your circumstances because he knows the real you. He also lets you be stubborn. But one thing that he will not do is let you stay in that state of mind. He delivered me from generational curses, myself, and the way of the world. I know him as "Jehovah Mephalti," my deliverer.

God allows you time to come to yourself so that you can make a conscious decision to choose Him or stay where you are. God will step in and give you a chance to choose him even after all the things you've been through. After all that God allowed in my life, I chose Him and his way! The things you are going through or have gone through are not meant to cause you harm, but they are meant to give you an expected end.

I had to learn that you can't compare your life to others.

God's purpose and plan for each of us is different. We must trust Him and learn from our rights and wrongs. That's how we grow to be the person He has called us to be. Even though life has been challenging for me, I know God is in control of it all. I have learned to trust the process that gets me from me and over to God. It has not been easy, but I am determined and trust God in all things. No matter how many times I fell, I got back up again through Christ that strengthens me. I trust God with my whole life, and I love him with all my heart. I have a heart after God, and I want all my ways to please him so that he will make every enemy be at peace with me. Even after all I have been through, I still thank God that I was afflicted.

The journey was necessary for me to become the woman God wants me to be to enhance his kingdom. Now I can tell the world of His goodness and all he has done for me! My heart and soul say Hallelujah! Thank you, Lord, for saving me!

I am God's Wonderful Woman.

ABOUT THE AUTHOR

Kimberly Harris is the founder and CEO of God's Wonderful Woman Inc., a program that empowers single mothers by providing financial and spiritual support. As a passionate servant of God, Kimberly is dedicated to making a difference in her community and beyond. Hailing from Indianapolis, Indiana, Kimberly also serves her hometown as a Notary Public. A devoted wife and mother of three, she holds an accounting degree and has over twenty years of experience in the field. In 2024, Kimberly embraced her divine calling and fully committed to ministry, founding and pastoring Water Walking Faith Worship Assembly in Indianapolis. At the core of Kimberly's life is her unshakeable faith in God, which guides her both personally and professionally. She is deeply committed to walking with integrity, embodying the values of the Christian faith in all that she does. Despite numerous trials, Kimberly is an inspiring testament to God's ability to overcome obstacles. Through her efforts, she continually inspires those around her, firmly believing that God can do anything but fail.

www.ingramcontent.com/pod-product-compliance
Lightning Source LLC
Chambersburg PA
CBHW050913160426
43194CB00011B/2384